JANUARY 05, 1995

DEAREST NENG,

MAY WE GAIN LESSONS AND COLLECTIVIZE
EXPERIENCES FROM THESE SHARING ON MID LIFING...
MENCHIE

COMING
TO
TERMS

WRITINGS ON MIDLIFE
BY 15 WOMEN

Edited by
Lorna Kalaw-Tirol

ANVIL PUBLISHING INC.

Published and exclusively distributed by
ANVIL PUBLISHING, INC.
3/F Rudgen II Bldg.
17 Shaw Boulevard
1600 Pasig, Metro Manila
Telephones 631-7048, 633-6121, 633-6136
Fax (632) 631-3766

©Lorna Kalaw-Tirol and
Anvil Publishing, Inc., 1994

First printing, March 1994
Second printing, November 1994

Cover and book design
by Joanne de León

Cover painting entitled "Self-Portrait" (1993)
by Barbara C. Gonzalez

Cover photograph
by Chito Madroño

National Library of the Philippines DIP data

Recommended entry:

Coming to Terms: writings on mid-life
    by 15 women / editor, Lorna Kalaw-Tirol.
    Pasig, Metro Manila: Anvil Pub., 1994.
    232 p.

1. Middle age - psychological aspects.
    I. Kalaw-Tirol, Lorna.

BF724.6 1994 155.66 P941000006
ISBN 971-27-0331-2

Printed by
Cacho Hermanos, Inc.
Pines & Union Sts., Mandaluyong, Metro Manila

For my parents, Jose (†) and Nelly Kalaw,
with love and gratitude

and for Vic, Jo-Ed, and Paulo,
with love and hope

CONTENTS

INTRODUCTION
Lorna Kalaw-Tirol

FOREWORD
Conrado de Quiros

TWENTY (OR SO) QUESTIONS
Bernardita A. Azurin, *1*

A MOST BEAUTIFUL FRIENDSHIP
Florina F. Castillo, *13*

A SECOND DEBUT
Gemma Guerrero Cruz, *33*

PRIVILEGE AND PAIN
Neni Sta. Romana-Cruz, *41*

DISABLED IN MENOPAUSE
Chic Fortich, *55*

ONE WITH THE UNIVERSE
Mariel N. Francisco, *69*

THE SPIRITUAL JOURNEY
Judette A. Gallares, r.c., *93*

THREE LETTERS
Margarita Go Singco-Holmes, Ph.D., *109*

IN THE MIDDLE OF THE ROAD TO ETERNITY
Marra PL. Lanot, *125*

MIDLIFE AMONG THE PEOPLE
Carolina S. Malay, *127*

JOURNEY AND ARRIVAL
Asuncion David Maramba, *135*

AN UNMARRIED WOMAN
Imelda M. Nicolas, *147*

LETTING GO: A WIDOW IN MIDLIFE
Alice A. Pañares, *155*

FREEDOM TO BE
Ma. Agnes O. Prieto, *175*

SEARCHING FOR ME
Tessie Tomas, *191*

THE WOMEN BEHIND THE BOOK

INTRODUCTION
LORNA KALAW-TIROL

THIS BOOK began four years ago as a midlifer's wish. Having gone through some of the mystifying angst that comes with entering one's forties, and having emerged from it whole and happier than I had ever been in a long time, I wanted other women to know that midlife is not a dead end, that it need not be the crisis that it is to many of us, that it can in fact be the best time of our lives. In this wish I was joined by a friend of almost thirty years, Judette Gallares, r.c., a Cenacle nun who specializes in ministry and counseling and with whom I have shared life's journeys — through beaux and jobs, marriage for me and the convent for her, my family, her community, our hysterectomies, our midlife struggles.

In one of the few long conversations we somehow manage to have despite distance and our disparate individual lives, Judette and I mulled the idea of a book on midlife. We didn't know then what form the book would take, only that it would be something that would help women through this period that Gail Sheehy has termed Second Adulthood. The idea remained a wish for three years since I didn't know the mechanics of writing a book and getting it published. Now and then, however, I would mention it casually to women friends and acquaintances who were themselves midlifers. Why not, they would say, it's about time something like it was written. By the time I met Karina Bolasco of Anvil, I knew what kind of book I wanted: intensely personal accounts on midlife by women in midlife. She was enthusiastic when I mentioned it to her, although I'm sure she gets excited about every book idea that comes her way. But she was not only encouraging, she was determined. Almost immediately she asked for a concept and a list of the writers I had in mind. There was no turning back. This was the generative phase of midlife Judette had told me about when she encouraged me to write again after years of just editing other people's work, for I had become unsure that I could manage even a good paragraph.

This book, therefore, is a new beginning for me in my midlife. It is not mine, however, my book; I have only put it together. I feel truly blessed to have found fifteen women who expressed no qualms about going public as midlifers, and more important, were willing to trust me with their most private selves. Many of them I have known for years, and some of them are my cherished friends. They have given me much, much more than I asked for, and I have learned immeasurably from them. I thank them for their thrust and for for the new bonding between us that *Coming to Terms* has made possible.

Judette Gallares agreed to do the spiritual perspective after she had finished her own book, her fourth, and before leaving on a journey to the Holy Land with a group of retreatants from the United States and the Philippines.

Lala Castillo, whose son and mine were winners in a contest for grade school writers ten years ago, gave me a book on the psychological and spiritual dimensions of midlife long before she submitted her essay. "It was a joy to write this," she said in a letter that came with what she called her "thesis." "It clarified a lot of things for me. You didn't only ask me to write an essay — you made me examine this time of my life for all the significances and nuances — and I'm so glad you did."

Agnes Prieto was a very young soldier's wife who wrote romantic short stories when I met her some twenty years ago at the magazine office where I worked. She has since gone through many lives, and many searchings. Her essay for this book, she said, "empowered" her and "made me aware of the power potential that arises from coming to terms with this phase in a woman's life."

Neni Sta. Romana-Cruz, a friend from way back and tireless promoter of children's literature, could have refused my invitation to be part of this book rather than go through the agony of recounting the many tragedies in her midlife. But here she is.

Asuncion David Maramba, for whom writing and editing books is both mission and avocation, insisted on writing her midlife manifesto. She may be past early midlife, she explained, but she is "still reeling from its effects."

Alice "Peanuts" Pañares had just been widowed when I first spoke of this project to her. Three years and a poignant essay later, she could write: "When I said yes to you, I never realized how soul-harrowing and difficult writing the article would be for me. I had to stop several times while writing it because the memory was like a knife opening old wounds that I thought had healed. Writing about the four years after Rau died, though painful, has been like a medicine. It has made me acknowledge all the pain, the woundedness of my soul, and it has healed and cleansed me. Thanks for forcing me to finally confront myself through this article."

Bernardita A. Azurin reveals in her contribution a funny bone I had not known existed. We had met each other briefly as campus journalists, and years later I did a magazine article on her as the young and aggressive publisher-editor of several agriculture publications. Berni could give Tessie Tomas competition should she decide, at the end of her ruminations on life's meaning, to shift gears.

Tessie Tomas herself, the picture of confident onstage, was reluctant to accept my invitation, but not because she was not willing to go personal. "Do I have a right to be in the book?" she asked nervously after being told the names of some of the other writers. After finishing her essay, however, as the reader will see from its ending, she felt confident enough to think about doing a book of her own.

Marra Lanot was in the midst of writing her poem when she lost her father, the respected writer and astrologer Serafin Lanot, and so it was understandable that the first poem she submitted should center on him. She bravely rose above her grief, however, and composed another.

Carolina "Bobbie" Malay, whose first reaction when invited to write was that she did not know what midlife was, would lose her own mother soon after she completed her piece. She had kept Ayi faithful company as the latter battled with the cancer that finally killed her. Ayi herself was a gentle friend and role model to me and to countless others who marvelled at her stamina and admired her grace and elegance and generous spirit, qualities Bobbie embodies too.

I was fortunate to catch Gemma Cruz between trips. She now shuttles between Manila and Mexico City for both business and personal reasons. Readers may be disappointed that the quintessential beauty queen, now a golden girl, chose not to disclose details about her own midlife, but there is a wealth of wisdom in her account and quite a bit contained between the lines.

Mariel Francisco just had to be in this book, not only because she is a marvelous writer but also because her personal experience of midlife, rich and multifaceted, deserves to be shared.

Chic Fortich, almost totally blind and deaf, did not balk when I asked her to find out how women with other kinds of disability are coping with midlife. It meant additional work for her, but she approached the assignment with her usual spunk and professionalism.

Imelda Nicolas was two years my senior at St. Theresa's, where she was an outstanding student and an outspoken and somewhat irreverent, and therefore refreshing, student leader. When told about this book, she expressed no reservations about writing as a confirmed single woman.

Margarita Holmes, who is temporarily based in North Carolina, USA, could not write an original article but sent in three letters previously published in her column in *The Manila Times*.

These fifteen women are extraordinary in their honesty and courage, in writing as they have — straight from the gut, and from the heart. It is, they will tell you, the only way to write.

I am honored, and deeply grateful, to be in their company.

THE COVER design could not be more apt. It was fortuitous that just as Joanne de Leon was beginning to work on studies for the cover, Barbara "Tweetums" Gonzalez was mounting her first show as an artist. That in itself was a midlife phenomenon. Here was an exceptionally talented woman who had already made her mark as president of a large advertising company and columnist and book writer, now proving that there was no end to her creativity, that Gail Sheehy was right — midlife is often the beginning of the most creative period in a woman's life.

The art Tweetums has created in her midlife is her distinctive contribution to this book. She was delighted to be told that her painting would be used on the cover. Is it really that good? she wanted to be assured. It is. But that was not the only consideration. Her self-portrait, of a woman casually attired in loose shirt and denims and looking confident and serene, could well be all the other women in this book.

FINALLY, I must thank Karina Bolasco for her faith in midlifing women, and her assistant, Ani Habulan, for her infinite patience. And to Conrad de Quiros, who gamely agreed to write the foreword for a book on women older than he (with the exception of one), the lifelong gratitude of this forty-seven-year-old. He has simply confirmed what his women readers have been suspecting all along — that he is at heart a ladies' man.

24 January 1994

TWICE CURST, TWICE BLEST

I DO NOT KNOW what madness persuaded the editor and contributors of this volume to implicate me in this plot. Everyone in it is a woman in her forties and fifties. I am forty-two and a man—or so last I looked. Maybe they figured one out of two isn't so bad.

But whatever their reasons, I am grateful for them. Reading the essays in this book has been an education for me in the most expansive, mind-blowing sense of the term. It has also been a source of boundless joy. These are not essays you read with a view to improving your mind. These are essays you read with a view to replenishing your soul. You do not walk through them blithely, and reach the end richer by one or two ideas, or remembrances. You sip them slowly, and feel the warmth of life tingle through your veins.

I came to this book prepared to do the first. I ended up doing the second. It was as much an immense curiosity as an immense friendship with Lorna Kalaw-Tirol that made me agree to write the foreword for this book. I thought it would be a unique opportunity to discover how women, particularly accomplished Filipino women, look at the world from the window of a fretful age. But I was to discover more about the object than the subject, the contemplatee than the contemplator, the gestalt of middle age than the psychology of women.

Women are not different from you and me. Middle-aged people are different from you and me. Or you and you. Me, I'm part of the tribe.

I say so proudly, after having traversed this once *terra incognita* with some of the best guides in the world. Dante could not have had a better Beatrice to hold his hand.

Several things make the essays in this book a precious find. Chief of them is that their authors are some of the keenest observers, some of the most self-aware persons I've come across in a long time. Stereotype that it is, it is not always untrue that women are more given to introspection than extrospection, to exploring the internal rather than external frontiers of life, to trying to change themselves than the world. In middle age, I've often wondered if Marxism wasn't sexist in its view that changes in the material world were all that mattered. The essays here, with their profound interiority, certainly seem to argue for the opposite.

A life unexamined, as they say, is a life unlived. If so, then these are lives deeply lived. For they have been examined with a ruthlessness comparable to the Inquisition itself. Happily, the results are not all moans and groans, which are all you hear from the rack. Some are cries of pain, others are shouts of exultation. At their best, they are neither of the two, or both. They are like the sobs of a mother at childbirth.

But the authors here are not just great meditators of life, they are great articulators of it. They are not just some of the most self-aware persons in the world, they are some of the best storytellers in it. It is easy to make a map of thoughts; it is not always easy to make a map of feelings. It is easy to draw the contours of events and experiences; it is not always as easy to draw the contours of pain and joy. The authors of these essays do not only make us see and hear their journey and their striving, they make us part of them. They make us part of their despair, they make us part of their triumph. They make us part of their emptiness, they make us part of their fullness.

If the authors are able to do so, it is not all because of verbal, or literary, prowess, however they are amply endowed with them. It is also because of a tremendous capacity for honesty and openness. Here is more than a baring of innermost thoughts. Here is a baring of innermost self. Here is more than nakedness to the marrow of the body. Here is nakedness to the marrow of the soul.

One is tempted to admire the courage or marvel at the bravado, but it is neither the one nor the other. There is something about the way these women describe their accomplishments and failures that is past boasting or humility. There is in it the need to say something urgent, something important, something necessary. A terrible secret, or discovery, or yearning, needs to be said, and must be said in the simplest way possible. Without embellishment, without coyness, without covering up. Strictly 20-20 vision, with but the slightest traces of gray or pink in the horn-rimmed eyeglasses.

You know that something has been reached when people can say these things. It is not that they no longer care what others will say about them. It is that they care to be known only for what they are. It is at once a feeling of caring and of not caring, both to an intense degree. It is not the not caring of being indifferent. It is the not caring of not wanting to be fettered by the definitions of a capricious—and quite male-dominated—world. It is not the caring of wanting to be noticed or approved of. It is the caring of wanting desperately to exist for oneself so that one can exist for others.

A paradox? Ah, but that is what midlife is all about. A paradox. Or so that is what comes across in these pages. It is the coming apart and coming together of things. There are paradoxes here enough to delight an incorrigible Zen Buddhist. As there are contradictions here enough to warm the heart of a playful dialectician. True understanding, physicists and mysticists say, lies beyond the barrier of paradox. If so, then the essays here bring us dangerously close to it.

Among the paradoxes of midlife that they reveal:

It is the worst time of all, it is the best time of all. It is a time of panic, of seeing the beginning of the end, of looking back and wondering if all that one was amounted to a hill of beans. But it is also a time of learning, of standing at the threshold of new things, of wondering if looking back and finding oneself wanting is not the most stupid thing to do. It is a time of finding old answers to new questions. It is a time of asking new questions to old answers.

It is a time of death, it is a time of life. The death is quite literal too. The smell of death hangs in the air—from disease, from the aching in the bones, from the death of parent, or husband, or sibling. They are all there. But it is a time too of discovering the utter preciousness of life. Ma. Agnes Prieto has found midlife not unlike the passage from adolescence to adulthood, with all its exciting and terrifying beauty. But the passage from adulthood into a new adulthood—a new adulthood that brings out the child in oneself again—is by far the more resplendent in its self-awareness.

Others discovered the preciousness of life in other ways. In midlife, Florina Castillo became closer to the nuns of her school who drew out their twilight years in profound serenity, and from them learnt the art of embracing life tightly while always being prepared to let go. In being alone and a widow, Alice Pañares came to know the depths of love and the true meaning of human relationships. Near-blind, Chic Fortich saw how her blindness really lay in more than the disrepair of her eyes. Like Tiresias before her, she saw—quite physically—how people who had eyes could be blind, and how people who did not could see. Everywhere there was blindness to the beauty around us, the beauty of caring and compassion and friendship.

These are not facile observations born of an adolescent need to sound profound, or be cute. Blindness and widowhood, and, yes, midlife do lend themselves to that. These are truths wrung from pain, like confessions from people in the throes of torture.

Yet there's more.

Midlife is a time of extraordinariness, it is a time of ordinariness. It is discovering the profundity of the commonplace and the commonplaceness of the profound. It is the fusing of—as E. Aguilar Cruz used to say—the sublime and the paralytic. Mariel Francisco defied rule and routine and saw the vastness of the spirit world in yoga and yoghurt. Asuncion David Maramba looked to her heart and learned to appreciate the things she had always taken for granted: friendships, family, old picture albums. Judette Gallares, r.c. emerged from her dark night of the soul to achieve new levels of religious ecstasy. Neni Sta. Romana-Cruz emerged from one family tragedy after another to achieve new heights of joy in living away from the madding crowd, and writing.

Midlife is a time of intense spirituality, it is a time of intense sensuality. It is a time of other-worldliness,it is a time of risqueness. It is a time of great discoveries in the wilderness of the soul. It is a time of great discoveries in the wilderness of the body. The women here do not merely talk of unearthly ecstasies; they talk, quite openly, of earthly ones. It is all of a piece. The liberation of the mind is the liberation of the body. The road that leads to cosmic orgasms is the same road that leads to seismic ones. The process that makes one a better person is the same process that makes one a better sexual partner.

Ask Margarita Holmes. She's the one who raises sex to the higher level of philosophy, and philosophy to the even higher level of sex. Indeed, ask Gemma Guerrero Cruz. She's the one who has discovered the plenitude of life not in Babette's feast but in something pretty close to it: the texture of dresses. "A long-sleeved nothing dress at first sight, it turned out to be sheer opulence on closer inspection. The chartreuse dress was lined with the purest printed silk, a burst of autumn foliage, such precious hedonistic details only the wearer could appreciate, or perhaps reveal in deepest intimacy. (Years later, as I strolled through my first autumn forest at Henley, it was the silk lining of that dress that suddenly flashed in my mind.)" That's sensuality of spiritual proportions.

Midlife is a time of freedom, it is a time of commitment. It is a time of great ego and self-centeredness, it is a time of great surrender and selflessness. It is a time of passionate individuality, it is a time of passionate communing — with nature, with society, with lover. Imelda Nicolas and Agnes Prieto found in singleness the depths of commitment. The other women found in the pit of marriedness the shaft of independence.

Tessie Tomas felt the need for love welling out from a welter of success and accomplishment. The others found the need for success and accomplishment welling out from the welter of love. In youth, Bernardita A. Azurin saw herself as the center of the universe; in midlife she still sees herself as the center of the universe but no longer agonizes over it. In youth, Bobbie Malay saw changing the world as the reason for her being; in midlife she still sees changing the world as the reason for her being, but no longer shouts slogans over it. Marra Lanot is adrift on a dance floor in a halfway house to eternity. Florina Castillo is rooted in a friendship — or mother-daughter relationship? — as wondrous and mysterious as middle age.

I could go on and on, but I will leave the reader to scour the terrain and discover its wonders for himself or herself. The book is filled with them. Suffice it to end by saying that the book itself, like its chosen subject, is a paradox. It is intensely personal, yet it is dazzlingly universal. It is the work of individual women in middle age — each word in the phrase, "individual," "women," and "middle age," holding a meaning all its own. But it is the very personal-ness of it that touches everyone, women and men, young and old, the hopeful and despairing, with the power and clarity of its convictions. The best confessions reach their apogee as truth.

This book, like its chosen subject, is the middle of things. It is the coming and going, it is the arriving and leaving, it is the closing and opening of doors. The middle is also the center of things. Maybe it's as T.S. Eliot says: At the end of our journey, we will go back to where we started and see the place for the first time. Or maybe it's just as the individual middle-aged women in this book say. In the end, it all comes down to this:

A woman in midlife is twice curst. A woman in midlife is twice blest.

TWENTY (OR SO) QUESTIONS

BERNARDITA A. AZURIN

How would you describe yourself in a 'personals' ad? Fortyish Asian female who looks but may not always act her age. With no pets, one husband, one son, and more than one friend. Communicator by profession, dabbler by choice. A passion for the arts and a weakness for sweet and tender hunks. Willing to try most anything once.

Engages in no-sweat pastimes — reading, watching movies, riding buses, counting bridges. Enjoys good food, good music, good company. Loves the mountains, the sea, and most living things. More spiritual than religious. More worldly than spiritual. Can be counted upon to stay through the tough times. Can also make the times tough.

Looking for real people who can become real friends. Sense of humor a must. Good looks not essential but may be an advantage. Fictitious characters will not be entertained.

How do you think your husband, son, and best friend would describe you?

My husband would refuse to describe me but if sufficiently intimidated would probably say I am "full of surprises, not all of them unpleasant." My son: "Her son's mother." My best friend: "Curious, in both senses of the word."

How would you like to be described?

Ten percent Mother Teresa, 10% Margaret Mead, 10% Lucille Ball, and 70% Dawn Zulueta.

Do you admit to being middle-aged?

I admit to being forty-six and feeling fabulous.

So can we assume that you are in midlife?

Can anything be closer to midlife than forty-six? Yes, you can assume I am in midlife. But . . . I may have passed the critical point.

What is the critical point?

It is when you cannot decide on whether the more interesting character in the movie "A Few Good Men" is Tom Cruise or Jack Nicholson.

When did this critical point hit you?

Summer of '85. I was thirty-seven going on thirty-eight. I had just come from a working stint abroad. I felt this strong need to bring down the curtain on Act I and set the stage for Act II.

I decided to go on a grand vacation, my first in decades, to give myself time to think things through. I would not hold down a regular job. I would instead take care of unfinished business, tie up loose ends. I would do the things I dreamt of doing if I had the time. I would give my life a dramatic turnaround.

If we can backtrack a bit, what was your life like before the

summer of '85?

Imperfect, just like everyone else's.

I was a middle child in a brood of seven so my parents left me pretty much alone. As a kid, I got along well with girlfriends but was high-handed with the boys. By the time I got interested in boys, they wouldn't give me the time of day.

In college, I was the worst combination of what a young person could be in the turbulent Sixties. I was a rebellious nerd, manic-depressive, obsessive-compulsive, ever in search of that elusive "speck of a meaning in a reality colored by meaninglessness."

After college, I worked for nine different outfits within seven years as either a writer, teacher, or editor. Within this seven-year period, I found the time to get married and bear a son.

When I was twenty-six, I decided I was good enough to be my own boss and for the next ten years, I ran a communications outfit publishing agri-aqua publications and managing special events. If you have been crazy enough to be self-employed, you will know that it is not a nine-to-five job and that you hardly ever take your hat off. That is what happened to me.

At the age of thirty-two, I discovered I had essential hypertension. I cannot understand why they call it that when I could do without it.

After the Aquino assassination, running a business in Manila became a nightmare. I decided to try my luck abroad. I went to Hawaii to work for an aquaculture consulting firm in Oahu. I stayed there for close to a year and never, never windsurfed.

Homesickness brought me back to Manila in the summer of '85.

So tell us about the summer of '85.

It was hot.

My son, who was fourteen years old at the time, joined me in a summer art course at the UP College of Fine Arts. I learned to do pencil portraits and did one of Tetchie Agbayani for the end-of-course exhibit. I forgot to take it home. It is the only creditable work of art that I have done and I don't even know where it is now.

I baked and sold chocolate chip cookies, coming up with my own

3

concoction after experimenting with about a dozen recipes. I collected hundreds of chicken recipes and tried out a few. Bear in mind that the creature doing all these things refused to look at the interior of a kitchen for years and was hearing the term "cookie sheet" for the first time.

I reread my favorite books, watched all sorts of movies, and wrote long, long letters to friends. I did needlework, tried to write some fiction and kept a journal of sorts. I did most of the household chores, having dispensed with the services of househelp that year. My blood pressure stayed at manageable levels. I kept my weight down. Life was wonderful.

I wasn't the only one to think it was a wonderful year. My husband took a picture of me that year and, out of the hundreds of pictures he had taken of me through the years, that was the picture he had enlarged and framed and then hung in his office. I don't know what this means but that framed picture is back in the house — it does not hang in his new office.

Before I could draw up the guidelines on how to proceed with my life, a work opportunity presented itself by year's end. Though reluctant at first, I eventually took it. I rejoined the work force, cut short my taking stock period and as Gail Sheehy would put it, left a "passage" uncompleted. It was all chaos, restlessness, desperation and boredom after that. Well, I exaggerate a bit. It was mostly muddling through after that.

The way you describe 1985, it does not sound at all like a bad year.

You're right. It was not. It was a wonderful year, one of my best, definitely. But I did not let it proceed to what I had hoped would be a graceful finish.

How did you feel during that "muddling through" period?

Terrible, with short episodes of terrific. As opposed to what I feel now, which is terrific, with short episodes of terrible.

I had a strong sense of discomfort, feeling ill at ease, not "at home." I had the impulse to start or end whatever there was to start or end but was unable to muster the energy to do anything. Immobilized is the word. At the same time, I felt restless. I had this need to escape. I wanted to buy a new wardrobe, grow a beard, change careers, set up house elsewhere.

I did not buy a new wardrobe nor grow a beard nor change careers. But I did set up house elsewhere a few times. My feelings did not change, however. I could have been lazing around in a luxurious villa in the south of France and I would have felt just as miserable. My problem was inside of me and the solutions offered by the outside world were of no help.

I felt that I had made a wrong turn somewhere and was hopelessly lost. Which reminds me. A few weeks ago, I came across a quotation which went, "No matter how far you have gone on the wrong road, turn back." Someone should have told me that a long time ago.

I know now that I should have faced my confusion like a woman and tried to understand it. But I kept evading it. So the crisis stayed and stayed and stayed. All of seven years. Now I tell my younger friends to stand up to their demons when they come. The act of exorcism is a necessity.

I still cannot get a clear sense of why you would call it a "muddling through" period.

Neither can I, but let me try to explain.

I felt like I was repeating myself. I was not moving forward at all. There was nothing new in my life. Whereas during my "sabbatical" I found out that I thoroughly enjoyed "artistic" activities, when I went back to work I engaged in exactly the same activities I was involved in during the previous ten years — starting up and running a publishing/special events management outfit.

On my forty-second year, a close friend invited me to join the government service. I took up the offer for several reasons. First, it was something new, hence different. Second, it would give me a chance to work with two of my bosom buddies. Third, for the first time in many years, I would not have the sole responsibility for what went on in an organization.

I worked in the bureaucracy for exactly three years and two months. It was this stint in government that precipitated the crossover. The routine, the lack of control soon got to me. This time, I was not just repeating myself. I was in a rut.

I would probably have been in a rut whether or not I was with the government. But the feeling was exacerbated by the fact that, as part of a monstrous bureaucracy, I did not believe my contributions were of much significance.

I made several attempts to quit my government job but it was only after attending a weekend seminar on personal empowerment in late July 1992 that I made the firm decision to really, truly quit. Two weeks after, I turned in my letter of resignation, which the big boss accepted with indecent haste. An unmistakable sign from heaven that it was time to move on.

I hope I am not giving the impression that my government job was the pits. Because it was not. I mean, not all throughout. In fact, I met some of the most wonderful human beings in the institution where I worked and whom I now count among my dearest friends. It's just that it was the wrong place for me to be in at that stage of my life.

Would you consider the act of resigning your crossover point?

In a way, yes. It was a symbol of sorts — that I was making a conscious and deliberate choice to close a chapter of my life. Deciding to resign made me feel that I was in charge of at least one aspect of my life even though it was not that significant an act. I mean, anyone can resign from a job. Resigning from being a wife or a mother would be a different matter altogether.

Shortly after I made the decision to resign, I was having coffee with this near-stranger who showed an inordinate interest in my past. As I began to tell him the story of my life, it dawned on me that there was a time when I was an interesting person. So where did this interesting person go? And why was I now walking around disguised as a fat and bored slob?

I looked into this stranger's face and found his smile enchanting.

I realized that my nerve endings were tingling. I was not dead. I could be touched and moved and respond to a gesture of tenderness.

Don't take my word for it. I am not one hundred percent positive that the episode I have just described happened in real life or at my alpha level.

So what has been happening to you since your encounter with this fascinating stranger?

Nothing earthshaking. Nothing that would show, except for the loss of a few unwanted pounds. I would say, however, that most of the changes have been inside of me. I no longer feel that I am at a dress rehearsal. I am right smack in the middle of a wacky play and relishing my role in it.

Even though one of the causes of my depression in the past was the fact that I felt I kept repeating myself, I got involved for the nth time in setting up another communications company right after my cross-over point. This means I am still doing the things I used to do but feeling much more positive about the experience.

What are the parts of you which you feel you can leave behind? Which would you consider unfinished?

Well, I did think at one point that I could leave parts of myself behind, like all the cellulite, and that I needed to pay attention to the neglected parts, whichever these were. But it is not that simple. I think it is more a sense of coming to terms with your whole self, of accepting what you are, warts and all. I have forgiven myself for whatever was "unsavory" in my past and would like memories of the good times to be part of my present.

My "unfinished business" has more to do with the "creative" part of me. I'd like to do more writing now, write more than just memos and concept papers.

I'm writing poetry again after a twenty-year hiatus. If you read the poems I've written in the last twelve months or so and compare them with those I wrote twenty years ago, you would not believe that these were written by one and the same person. The poems I wrote in the late Sixties and early Seventies were thoroughly cynical. The ones I am writing now show that I'm willing to admit to a little vulnerability. I thought like a bitter old woman when I was young, and now that I am middle-aged, I think like a young girl in the throes of first love. Is it possible that I am in love? Or am I just schizophrenic?

Are you saying that you are ecstatic about middle age?
Heavens, no. My feelings are ... well ... ambivalent. Most of the time I am comfortable with the feeling. But when I read the classifieds on Sunday and find that nobody wants to hire a person past thirty-five, I realize that maturity and broad experience are not all that in demand. Thank God I'm not looking for a job. My son certainly stands a better chance of finding employment than I do.

How would you describe your present self?
Okay in general. I like myself better although some of my friends swear I have grown more obnoxious. Who cares? The hormonal changes taking place within my body are probably making me more tolerant of my weaknesses. My friends' hormonal changes, on the other hand, may be clouding their judgment.

I am less panicky, with a higher tolerance level for brownouts, traffic jams, and other aggravations of life. I have fewer fears. I'd still go ahead and do what I believe needs to be done, even if people think I'm crazy.

I am closer to my family and enjoy their company more. Again, the feelings may not necessarily be mutual. The friends I keep in touch with on a regular basis are fewer and more precious.

I feel free. I find myself laughing and smiling more these days, in a playful mood most of the time. I can't take myself too seriously.

A few weeks back, I attended this personality development seminar where we were asked to tell the group what we felt were our best assets. When I stood up and said "I don't take myself too seriously," the facilitator looked puzzled. She could not understand how anyone could consider that a positive trait. But then she was not middle-aged.

Are you serious?
Are you serious?

I mean, are you serious about not taking yourself too seriously?
Of course. You see, when I was younger, I never thought I'd live beyond age forty. I saw myself as Camille dying from consumption and true love at the age of thirty-three. I am well past forty now and still alive and well so I feel that from here on I'm living on bonus time.

I am less afraid of dying now than, say, ten years ago. Perhaps because a number of my contemporaries have passed away. Just last December, a childhood friend died suddenly from an aneurysm. Shortly after, a classmate from high school succumbed to a heart attack. She was just seeing her Australian husband off at the airport. She herself was preparing to immigrate to Australia in a few months. And in the last two years, I've had a couple of near-death experiences which I'd rather not go into.

If you hear stories like these and if you read the obits every day like I do, you can't help but feel grateful for being alive and be determined to live every single moment of your life. Sounds corny but it's true.

What is different about you now from what you were twenty years ago?
A lot. When I was young, I thought of myself as the center of the universe. Every time I walked down the street, I was positive everyone had his or her eyes on me. I was terribly self-conscious.

Now that I am older, I still think of myself as the center of the universe but I no longer agonize over it. I am less concerned about what other people think of me. I can tell a man he has a magnificent physique without worrying that he will think I am lusting after him. That would be his problem.

Another difference is my perception of time. When I was young, I felt I had all the time in the world for just about anything I wanted to do. All-night parties were no big deal. Now I tend to be more

9

discriminating when it comes to activities. Not too much TV. Not too much partying. Not too much "malling."

At the same time, I am not as future-oriented as I used to be. I can do something for its own sake. I can waste time without feeling guilty about it. Be here now, says Ram Dass. I am inclined to follow his advice.

What do I have now that I didn't have then? Experience, which has given me more poise — uh-huh, more self-possession — uh-huh, and a broader perspective about the world in general.

But, you see, you are only asking what is different about me now. You should also ask what has not changed about my life, because in one sense nothing has changed. My personal world is still pretty much what it was ten years ago. What has changed is my viewpoint. I am now looking at the world through a new pair of bifocals.

You sure sound upbeat, but there must be something you absolutely hate about middle age.

Well, I could do without the double chin, saddle bags, grey hair, failing eyesight, wrinkles, liver spots, hormonal imbalances, etcetera, etcetera.

What are the things you did right?

Getting married at a young age and having my baby in my early twenties. Now he is all grown, the spitting image of his father, even though both father and son deny it. He is finished with school and earning his own keep. I am very proud of him and I adore him. Especially when he sends me his personalized funny cards on "no-occasion" occasions and buys me a gallon of Selecta ice cream on weekends.

Do you have any major regrets?

Getting married. Just kidding, sweetheart.

I am happy to report that all of my regrets are minor.

What is your attitude towards relationships?

10

I don't have much to say about relationships at this point. This probably means that I have been giving the subject too much or too little thought. What I can say is I will honor whatever commitments I have made in the past but am open to making new ones.

When you were young, what did you think you would look like in middle age?

Worst-case scenario? Like Raquel Welch at age thirty-three.

Where do you see yourself twenty years from now?

I cannot see and I cannot say. I'd love to surprise everyone, though, including myself.

What do you look forward to?

A good night's rest, with pleasant dreams, and waking up to a new day.

A MOST BEAUTIFUL FRIENDSHIP

FLORINA F. CASTILLO

S HORTLY AFTER the schoolyear opened last June, I received, scribbled at the back of a lovely photograph of dawn on a beach, this poem written by a former pupil now come home again to me:

Dawn creeps into this tiny chamber
Kept with care and thoughts of you
Warming sunshine now reminds me
Of that first dawn we saw
Together.

Deeply touched, I answered her back thus:

When we saw that first dawn together
How far away
Midday
Or the sunset

Seemed to be
I did not look
Beyond the dawn
I saw unfolding in your eyes.

Strange, is it not, that when you're twenty or thirty, forty seems so far away. Then suddenly, without your even noticing it, you're forty-five, forty-eight.

And you don't even notice the almost full circles you seem to be making all the time. And the feeling that with you all of life is making one long, graceful pirouette so that at last you can touch the tips of your toes without losing your balance or your grace.

I didn't know what midlife was all about when it started to happen to me. What I remember now is wondering why a strange thought seemed to keep coming back to me with a strange regularity I could not explain. It was a thought that was a question and it always came to me in the morning. I was later to notice that it came just before my monthly period. Strangely, it would come when I was in front of the mirror combing my hair. I'd look at myself in the mirror and from somewhere something would nag me, saying, "Where have all the years gone, Lala?" And maybe for a second or two, I'd feel a wave of regret come over me, a kind of grieving for things that might have been.

My household, however, is a three-ring circus at this hour in the morning, and so I really never had the luxury of indulging in this kind of feeling for too long. And never really bothering to find out where all my precious years had gone, I'd go off to school and attend the six-ring circus that is the grade school of which I happen to be the principal. As soon as I'd seen the first toothy little girl smile of the schoolday, I really couldn't care less about where the years had gone. Life was full. And happy. And busy. I had no time to sit and wonder where the years had gone. Or so I thought. Till my first big midlife experience happened in a most unexpected way.

IT WAS 1989. I was forty-five. And for the first time in my life, I suffered a broken friendship.

Perhaps what you must first know is that I work in a school for girls, have been working in the same place (where I also studied) for more than twenty-five years.

Now when you're a school person, you deal almost all day with thought and feeling, and in a grade school you often deal more with feeling than with thought. Many of our faculty development sessions are human development sessions. And so, while they aim at making us work in greater harmony with one another, they also make us more vulnerable to one another. Furthermore, we live in an almost manless world. The only men on campus are a few male teachers, the security guards, the drivers, the janitors, and the gardeners (bless them!).

Among ourselves, we developed long standing friendships, some deep, some shallow, some spontaneous, and some by force of circumstance. You had to be friends if you belonged to a secretarial pool or to a teaching team or to a management team. You didn't have much choice, really. We often sat at table together, then clawed each other's eyes out afterward.

But we also developed deep friendships that partook of the best of our professional and personal selves. These were the friendships that were born of shared tasks and shared commitments. They were beautiful friendships that blossomed across faculty rooms and conference tables, beautiful boss-subordinate, tutor-tutee, collegial relationships that often invited an exquisite kind of growing in each other's presence. Beautiful friendships among women engaged in such a noble task as education.

While our friendships were genuine and beautiful, however, they were also beleaguered by the midlife changes that we seemed to be going through almost at the same time. It was no joke to go through midlife in the company of fifty other women who were midlifing as well.

And so my midlife "officially" and dramatically began when a friendship such as I have described earlier gave way.

It was a friendship of almost fourteen years with someone who till that time had shown me nothing but affection, understanding, and generosity.

It does not matter now what the quarrel was about. What matters in the looking back is how the experience of that broken friendship ushered me into midlife.

As I wrote in my poem, when you're twenty, thirty, forty and midday seems so far away.

I had a wonderful husband, four equally wonderful children, a happy home, and a good job. Life was happy and heady; my husband and I were at the peak of our careers. We weren't rich, but we weren't poor, either. We were happy and that was all that mattered.

I went up the organizational ladder without even trying to. I never wanted to be a grade school principal, never thought I'd ever be that. Yet, given the job, I discovered that I could be good at it. I liked it, after all. I liked seeing an idea grow in the hands of many people. I liked the demands that curriculum development imposed on my creativity. I could live with the many ambiguities and the tentativeness of a grade school administrator's life. Most of all, I loved the little girls and I liked the seasons in a school — beginnings, endings, vacations, back-to-school days, graduations.

I had been a grade school principal for about seven years. And thanks to a school president who allowed me to try my wings in many directions, I had done many things no other grade school principal had done. I knew I enjoyed the respect and admiration, and maybe the envy, of colleagues in the field. Even the doubting Thomases who gasped, "But she's an artist. She can't make a good principal!" had to eat their words as I blithely proved them wrong.

The grade school I ran rang with the laughter of happy children. I took children to the deep ravine-villages and the steep mountain terraces of the Cordilleras in reckless pursuit of the Ifugao epic, the *Hudhud,* as it is chanted by Ifugaos at harvest time. I took teachers to the tip of Cotabato, to the T'bolis of Lake Sebu, and to the Badjao graveyards of Santa Cruz Island in Zamboanga. One young teacher once told me, "I'm so tired. You make my dreams come true so fast."

I was like a jet-propelled fire engine running at high gear all the time. No problem occupied me for too long. There was always a solution. And there was always tomorrow.

Perhaps I could think that way because I knew I was loved. Maybe I'm a late bloomer, but doors opened so easily to me. I had never in my life really experienced rejection or oppression. Everywhere I went, I was someone's beloved friend or daughter.

Then this friendship, whose lastingness I never questioned, suddenly gave way. The experience shook my Pollyanna kind of faith in the foreverness of things. For the very first time in my life, I realized that *all things must end.*

And then I learned to live alone with pain. I never thought that an emotional ache could bring on physical pain as well. I literally lived with an aching heart! And I had to live through it alone. Much as people loved me, no one else could ache for me. The only way I found to ease my pain was to write poetry. Every day I wrote poetry. Surprisingly, this time I wrote better poetry in Filipino than in English. To my great amusement, friends who read my poetry, not knowing for whom it was meant or the circumstances that gave it birth, thought it was excellent love poetry, found it, of all things, intense and passionate. I never bothered to explain to them that it was meant for another woman, for someone whom they all knew to be as prosaic and pragmatic as a flat tire.

I missed my friend very much. Suddenly, I wanted to tell her all the things I had left unspoken all those years we were friends.

I found myself looking out for her along the corridors, in the chapel, along the driveway I was like an adolescent running after her first crush.

For a full year, I lived through a kind of limbo which I blamed on this falling away. Some days I didn't want to go to school. I'd change clothes two or three times, choosing clothing that carried my friend's favorite color or design or which evoked some significant memory that we shared. Every day began with the hope that I might somehow bump into her and ended with the expectation that she might call that night. Everything in my life seemed to center on my lost friend who was also so deep in midlife she couldn't care less what happened

17

to me.

The worst thing about it was that through it all I had to keep my dignity and my bearing. I couldn't imagine myself going around like a lovelorn adolescent mooning over a lost friendship, as I carried out my administrative duties. I needed to be dignified, sane (or seemingly so) and agonizingly typical. Unfortunately or fortunately, this was the year I had to steer the grade school through an accreditation process. Work was good. It kept me sober and restrained. In spite of the turmoil inside me, I could present a calm and happy front.

But it was a strain on me — this need to appear composed, happy, and fulfilled while I was hurting like hell.

And then, perhaps because the context of our friendship and our falling away was our work in the school, I felt a growing disenchantment with my work. For the very first time in my life, I who never questioned anything about the school suddenly saw cause to raise questions I never would have had the courage to raise before.

Looking back now, I see that nothing had really gone wrong with the school. It still had the same culture, the same subculture, and the same counterculture I was always up in arms against. But bereft of the camaraderie of a colleague, for the first time in my life I asked myself, "Why stay?"

Later on, I would realize that this disenchantment and what I mistook for the courage to question were all part of a bigger, all embracing process of disengagement, which, quarrel or no quarrel, would probably have happened anyway. It was a slow weaning away from the old, familiar things meant to free me to explore other possibilities I had not considered until then.

AT ABOUT THIS TIME I was gifted with another friend who would help me through this process of disengagement and bring me to a happy reengagement with dreams I had long ago put aside in favor of more pragmatic pursuits.

She is a Renaissance person, a wonderful woman of such myriad facets whose presence in my life is an education in itself.

She is Naty Crame Rogers, a grande dame of the legitimate stage.

18

At seventy, though retired as professor emeritus of the Philippine Normal University, she remains active in the theater both as actress and as educator. To young and aspiring actors and actresses, she is a symbol of the achievements and accomplishments in the field that one might claim at seventy. And the story of her life might well be a history of Philippine theater.

She came into my life when I asked her to direct a pageant for the grade school.

Let me call her Tita Naty, the name by which she has become known to the hundreds of little girls in my school whose lives she has touched with a master's hand.

Between her and me blossomed an exquisitely beautiful friendship that has enriched both our lives, each of us finding in the other a new and perhaps poetic reason for living. Before we knew it, our families were sharing the friendship with us.

Her coming into my life brought about a great shift from task to meaning. Not that I did not find meaning in the things I did before she came. But till then the meaning seemed to stop when the project did and there were very few to share it with me. I wanted to be able to communicate the meaning I saw and felt and savored with someone who would see and feel and savor it with me.

I was looking for someone who would share with me, with the same ease and intensity, the price of Magnolia dressed chicken and the silence of a starlit night. I wanted to be able to share Shakespeare with someone while I was putting on my nylons or making a julienne of bell peppers. I wanted to indulge in Elizabeth Barrett Browning's "feeling out of sight for the ends of Being ..." while on my way to the canteen to buy fishballs. And I realized that in midlife it was not enough to have an understanding husband and loving children and a job that paid well. Somehow, the human heart hungered for more.

I don't know if I'm just different, but I am obsessed with the meaning of meaning. For me, this obsession found fulfillment in the company of another woman, in a deep relationship that was not hampered or complicated by heterosexual overtones. We were just two human beings relating, touching base with each other. The fact

19

that we were both women gave our friendship a strong, dynamic but distinctly feminine aura.

The manner in which we wandered into each other's lives is one of the most beautiful milestones in my midlife and carries with it a mystical quality I cannot quite explain.

It was the summer of 1990, a year after my broken friendship. After a backbreaking schoolyear spent preparing for an accreditation visit, I thought the faculty would welcome a different kind of summer workshop. I thought the teachers needed a respite from all the paper and pencil work they had been doing all year.

Also, a labor union was in the process of being formed. I thought the experience of working together on a stage production might revitalize the faculty's flagging morale. I asked Tita Naty to give the entire grade school faculty a summer drama workshop.

In the tradition of setting a good example for my teachers, but more because I really like to act, I joined the production myself. I was to play a small role as Narcisa, the sister of Jose Rizal, in Severino Montano's "The Love of Leonor Rivera." For that role, Tita Naty lent me a beautiful Maria Clara costume that belonged to her, along with a pretty, old-fashioned hand-embroidered chemise.

Since I was very busy, I found the time to try on the costume only the night before the gala performance. It was a cold and rainy night. I had not gotten beyond the chemise when I felt a strange warmth envelop me, as though someone had held a strong incandescent lamp about half a foot away from me. I hurried through the rest of the costume filled with awe and wonder. That very night I wrote Tita Naty: "I'm not a great actress. But you are. I know nothing can go wrong tomorrow because I'm wearing the clothes of a great actress." Aura. That's what it must have been. The aura of someone whose lifetime has been dedicated to one all-consuming endeavor. That was the start of my fascination with this woman.

In the course of that memorable summer, as I kept her company every day at lunch, we shared thoughts and insights on literature and life, on teaching and education, and oh so many other things. How our minds met in beautiful complementation! Everything, somehow,

20

in my mind and heart seemed to have an echo in her own. And everything in her mind and heart likewise seemed to find some kindred thought or feeling in mine. Often we would laugh, realizing we were about to say the same thing at the same time. We would talk twenty-five hours a day.

We found ourselves trying to gift each other with a past we did not share. That was when I realized the importance of documentation. Suddenly, old photographs made sense. How did I look as a child? How did she look at sixteen? As a young stewardess? As a young actress? We would spend hours poring over old albums, enjoying every moment.

More than that, we enjoyed exchanging professional articles we had written and countless papers we had delivered several decades apart, marveling at how our thoughts, as they spanned several years of educational thinking, still dovetailed so strangely. This, of course, was the higher bond. If our personal lives and interests made us friends, our professional histories and our great love for scholarship and the academe made us colleagues. We shared the same intense love for the humanities, the same respect for research, the same sense of adventure in educational innovation. Often it was like a "naming game." I had the practice, she had the theory and the name for it. And vice versa. We were soul mates all the way.

We were both writers. Because we never seemed to have an end to the thoughts we shared, we wrote each day voluminously — notes, poems, journals, letters. And when our writing seemed in danger of getting lost under the mountain of papers we both keep, we decided to shuttle journals between us.

Later on, we learned that we could sit beside each other in comfortable silence for just as long. Faster than it would ordinarily have taken others, we forged strong bonds between us. And it did not take too long before we embarked on a spiritual journey together.

It seemed logical that we would relate on a mother-daughter plane, considering the years and generations between us. She was my mother's exact age and, by some twist of fate, we discovered that they (my mother and she) had been playmates.

I am an eldest child and an only daughter, seven brothers following me. My mother and I were great friends but I lost her early. She was only 54 when she died. I was on a semestral break then and engrossed in making class schedules for a new semester. Only later did I realize that I did not cry or mourn for my mother. At that time, I thought it was a show of strength and courage not to have mourned. Friends congratulated me for being so brave. I ignored the fact of my bereavement and turned to schoolwork and the urgent task of keeping alive a very sickly second son. I was kept busy trying to be strong for everybody else.

When I met Tita Naty, all that starch gave way. Here was someone to whom I could be a daughter again. Never having had a daughter of her own, she allowed me to indulge in the little mother-daughter frivolities I had enjoyed so much with my mother — things like wearing identical outfits or going window shopping together and instituting private little rituals like keeping happy secrets between us. I enjoyed asking her to button up my back (I'm very fond of dresses with about a hundred loop buttons at the back) or being looked over before I made the many "public appearances" a grade school principal must make, or being told "to call up as soon as you get home" as though I were a sixteen-year-old out on her first date. Little did people know that the grade school principal who shook their hands with such composure at a general assembly or a gala night had indulged in a hurried mother-daughter good-luck hug behind her office doors before coming out to meet them. It was good to feel like a child again. In fact, it felt good to know that I was tied to someone's apron strings all over again.

Maybe the psychologists have a term for it. I only know that in those affectionate mother-daughter transactions were the tears I did not shed for my mother.

Tita Naty, I found out, was so like my mother and yet so unlike her. For example, my own mother was a homemaker who taught me that "only bad girls wear makeup." The very first thing Tita Naty the stage actress taught me was how to put on makeup correctly. After that, she was able to convince me to dye my hair, something I had considered until then just a little bit short of promiscuity. She scoffed good-naturedly at my "Victorian ways" while I feigned shock at the slits on her skirts and her bright red nail polish.

Yet, unlike my mother, she came closer to what I wanted to be and to do at this stage of my life. No, not the slit skirts and the bright red nail polish, but drama, poetry, literature.

I was an English major. As a young girl, poetry, literature, campus journalism, and school dramatics were my life. I lived with ink on my fingers and if I wasn't in the printing press, I was rehearsing on the school stage.

At the end of high school, the results of my college aptitude tests baffled everybody. I remember the guidance director telling me, "This paper shows that you are highly artistic. It should tell you that the best career for you would be in the arts."

"But," she continued, her eyes peering at me as though she could see right through my entrails to Kingdom come, "this other sheet of paper tells me you want to be a truck driver. Can you explain why, Florina?"

Well, I was given the tests three times. And each time I still scored extraordinarily high in aesthetics *AND* I still wanted to be a truck driver.

So when I graduated from college at age nineteen, with all the glory of a cum laude behind me, I still didn't know what I wanted to be: poet, journalist, or theater person. I swore I would never be a teacher. But that's exactly what I became. A teacher. An ordinary grade school teacher. My role models? Julie Andrews and Mary Poppins.

I guess if there's any career that might combine aesthetics and truck driving, it is teaching.

My first assignment was to teach language arts and reading to fourth and seventh graders. I learned to put aside the problem of evil in Greek tragedy and left Hector and Andromache at the Skaian Gate to do SRA and spelling drills and penmanship exercises. For a while, though, I clung tenaciously to my dreams and clandestinely allowed Gerald Manley Hopkins and Shakespeare to sneak into my reading classes.

Little by little, in spite of myself, I obediently fell into the mold of a "good" teacher, putting my college training at the service of the grade school. I moderated the school paper, taught TESL (Teaching English as a Second Language), and without any formal training, was on call for every school production. But I was restless. I wanted to do something exciting. I thought there must be more to life than faculty meetings and lesson plans. I found myself resigning at the end of every blessed schoolyear.

I tried a job as a promotions writer but I couldn't see myself selling the *Manila Chronicle* eight hours a day for the rest of my life.

I enrolled in a master's program in theater arts at the Ateneo but gave that up when I got married. (I'm probably the only bride on record who took an exam in acting on her wedding day.)

Back in St. Scholastica's Grade School after I got married, I buckled down to the serious task of earning a living and starting a family.

Starry-eyed and lovestruck, I laid my dreams neatly away and put heart and soul into the task of education and school administration. I have been in school administration for twenty-three years now, first as assistant to the principal for academic affairs and then as grade school principal.

It was still aesthetics and truck driving. But more truck driving, really.

I learned to assign teaching loads, make teaching schedules, interpret standardized test results, work out faculty recruitment and evaluation procedures. Surprisingly, I enjoyed the technical aspects of the job as well as its creative aspects. And I like to think I did pretty well in both areas. People said I was a good principal. If I was, it wasn't because I was good at truck driving but because I went at the principalship the way I would write a poem.

For more than twenty years, I was deep in parenting and school management. My four children were born four years apart of one another, so for sixteen years it seemed like I always had a baby and a toddler on my hands. While I buried myself in management literature, I never once held a novel again except for Don Quixote which I read to my son Gaby whenever I had to climb into the oxygen tent with him. The only times I still got to read and write poetry were those occasional writing workshops for children that I conducted twice or thrice a year. In the meantime, I smuggled my babies into Balcony II of the Cultural Center to watch a ballet, learning to watch "Swan Lake" while making sure my son didn't fall off the balcony at the same time. That and a few PETA presentations at Fort Santiago (in summer, when the *yaya* was on vacation) were all the theater I knew in those years.

My feats as wife and mother notwithstanding, I was blazing trails where I was. I went around the country giving seminars in management skills for school administrators, interdisciplinary teaching, justice, peace and human rights education. By the time of the EDSA Revolution, I was at the forefront in the social studies area, pushing frontiers until the defense minister accused me of brainwashing children.

I did not realize how far away I had gone from the things that really gave me joy. Literature. Poetry. Not to teach but to fill my heart with song. Writing that wasn't just educational research or ghostwriting. And the theater, of course.

Tita Naty's coming to my life was like opening a hope chest and running my fingers lovingly over linen sewn and gathered in girlhood for someday. In such a beautiful way, my someday had come.

In school, with her help, I established not just a curriculum-based theater season that brought the classics within the joyful reach of children but also a Children and Teachers' Theater that put children and their teachers onstage together. Finally, Nick Joaquin and Shakespeare's "A Midsummer Night's Dream" became legitimate parts of our reading curriculum. It was a dream of more than twenty years come true.

What was fortunate, perhaps, was that this reengagement with old dreams did not run counter to my job or to my tasks in the first half of my life. My great joy lay in being able to bring the humanities, literature, and drama into the elementary classroom and to include an artist in the landscape of the school. As I read current educational literature and see trends moving towards the humanities and the arts, I know that I am moving in the right direction, the highlights of mid-life superimposed with beautiful congruence on all that I have been and all I had tried to build before it.

But outside the school were even more exciting "firsts" for me.

Last year, under the tutelage of Naty Crame Rogers, I not only translated two plays into Filipino but also saw them staged at the CCP's Huseng Batute Theater. I even played a major role in one of them. As I write this, I am deep in rehearsals for Tita Naty's Sala Theater production of Nick Joaquin's "A Portrait of the Artist as Filipino" where I'm playing Paula. My friends and I are members of Tita Naty's Philippine Drama Company, which specializes in Sala Theater and works with people like myself who enjoy acting but could never take it up as a career.

I am getting enviable training in different phases of theater work, as it were, and while sitting at a master's feet! Who would think life would give me such a gift twenty years after I sadly dropped out of that theater arts course I began at the Ateneo?

If schoolwork added spice to my life, this was like wine.

Then, after ten years of procrastinating, I decided to begin my doctoral studies, enrolling with Tita Naty at the University of Santo Tomas. The first course we took was on Shakespeare. I was like a fish in water! But when the first midterm exam came along, the ten years of hibernation told on me. I couldn't seem to remember a thing! I remember telling myself that if I passed that first midterm, I'd offer a Thanksgiving Mass. "Happy" is too mild a word to describe how I felt when, after two weeks, I was told that I scored the highest in class.

But I guess it wasn't just Shakespeare or experiencing success as a student again. To me, what mattered more was the joy of walking across the UST campus hand in hand with a friend and being able to talk Shakespeare in the car on the way home.

After Shakespeare came courses on Nobel Prize winners and the literature of India. This semester it is concepts of Asian drama and creative writing.

Soon my weekends became the most exciting days of my life. My husband and my children generously allowed me to spend Friday evenings with Tita Naty. The very act of packing for Friday night thrilled me no end. On Friday morning I'd go to school with my overnight bag packed, as eager for the dismissal bell to ring as the giddiest girl on campus. If there was something worthwhile in the theaters, then off we would go. If not, it was home to Aming Tahanan (that's what the Rogers home is called) to sit in the kitchen and talk more drama and theater while Tita Naty cooked supper. Then we'd go to bed and stay up late still chatting like two schoolgirls. On Saturday mornings we'd spend an hour or so in bed, still talking literature and life. I never could tell where our Saturday morning conversations would lead, but more often than not I would get a lecture on theater or acting or English teaching. The lovely four-poster bed where we slept became an extension of graduate school. After school, we'd go back to her home and my husband would pick me up, much like a boy fetching his girlfriend from a convent school dorm.

Maybe it was the change of activity and the change of roles. For twenty-four hours at least, I was not a grade school principal or a wife and mother. There were no decisions to make, no responsibilities to carry out, no domestic, mundane concerns to jar what I fondly call my "mountain moments," moments of soft and sweet surrender to the more lyrical qualities of life, moments when I seem able to gently touch truth and beauty and goodness in the resonance of a whisper, in the sheen of a word unspoken, or in a gentle "Come, sit beside me, let us read this book together." Moments when I am child and woman both. And I come home to my family a happier wife and mother for those brief eternities apart.

In these "brief eternities" in the presence of an artist-teacher, I learned the fullness of meaning. I discovered the great power of the sense of touch. I learned to stop for beauty. I learned to live one day at a time, to welcome joy or pain or sadness and while I savored these with a poet's tongue, to know they were gifts that will not last forever. I learned to hold life and all its gifts dearly but loosely.

And the realization that all things must end, that all I might have is the present and no more, became a new context and a new given in my life.

MY WORLD grew bigger than it had ever grown before. Not in terms of meeting new people or going places, but in terms of relating more intimately with others. In terms of knowing them and touching their lives and allowing them to touch my life.

Among my peers, however, I was often frustrated. For most of them were not comfortable with relationships beyond an occasional retreat sharing or a shopping spree at some Midnight Madness sale.

I found myself gravitating towards older people. I started to develop very deep friendships with nuns who had been college deans and former teachers and superiors and were now retired or almost retired. I found that I was more fulfilled and happier with them than with my peers. Strangely, in the sunset of their own lives, these nuns seemed to seek me out and to find joy in moments spent with me. In the middle of a working day, they would drop by my office just to say hello or call me by intercom just to ask me to lunch with them. Suddenly, many of my commitments to professional organizations did not seem as important as being with them.

With them, I stopped running for a while and learned to listen. I learned to listen to memories and the past. Sitting at the feet of women who had given their lifetime to education, I experienced a new kind of pedagogy, what I call the pedagogy of presence and remembrance.

I sought out the old sisters and asked them to relate to me little known stories in the school's eighty-seven-year history. My Scholastican heritage seemed all the more precious when seen through their eyes. And, disenchanted though I was with the school's present, I learned to cherish and value its past as I listened to them.

I sat beside their sickbeds, bringing to them my joys and my laurels as well as my heartaches in school administration, knowing that if there was anyone who would understand me, it was they. With my

28

hand in theirs, I listened to how they had lived through similar moments in their own administrative lives, seeing beautiful parallels and God's loving hand in stories still unmarred by senility or self-interest.

My trips to Baguio now never seemed complete without a visit to the little cemetery at the back of the convent, where, for a little while, I could sit in quiet communion with teachers long since gone and, steeped in the past, find meaning and a reason for living in the present. Baguio was not Baguio without an afternoon's quiet conversation about Christianity or the monastic life or what it means to be a Benedictine with one or the other old sisters.

Here was where the doors Tita Naty opened to me in human relationships opened full swing. Learning from her how beautiful the sense of touch could be, I who had never been "touchy" in my life learned to touch old people. I learned to embrace and kiss the old sisters and to allow them to kiss and embrace me as well. You must remember that many of them were German and had brought me up thinking that signs of affection were taboo. I was to discover that they were different in their old age. I revelled in the affection that I was everybody's little girl all over again. Sometimes, with great pride that warmed my heart, even those who had never been my teachers staked a claim to me.

To me, this was the meaning of life. Of being a child. Of growing up and growing old. The eternal child in me rose to meet with heart uplifted the eternal child in teachers with tough minds and tender hearts teaching even when they could no longer see or walk or even talk. I was learning about life from the best teachers, from those who were teaching themselves to say good-bye to it. For the first time in my life, I learned to look at death as a part of life.

Away from the madding crowd, the sisters gave me peace and love and taught me now to seek "the hermitage within." This was the meaning of meaning. And the moments spent with them became the oases of my days.

Yet sharply, as with Tita Naty, I was always aware that time spent with them was borrowed time.

29

I wrote a poem about this once. I called it "At the Doorway" and it began like this:

Let me linger
Just a little longer
In this moment
Spent with you.

And it ended with
This moment
May never come again.

Deep and exquisitely beautiful, these friendships with those to whom sunset and evening have so gracefully come, are preparing me to meet my own evening and sunset. I guess I am being better prepared for aging than I was ever prepared for midlife.

I have talked so little about my family. When I talk like this, I see eyebrows dangerously raised. And I know people wonder about my family and how they must feel. Thank God midlife happened when my children were grown, my eldest in his twenties and my youngest in her teens. And thank God for a husband who can understand what I was and still am going through, a husband who through twenty-four happy years has daily given to me the gift *to be.*

I remember how, coming home after my first weekend away, I rushed into the kitchen and started to cook as though my life depended on it. My eldest son came to me, put his arm around my shoulder and whispered with a smile, "Ma, don't try so hard." That's how wonderful and how generous my family can be.

I began this essay with a poem about the dawn. I shall end it with another poem. This one has a funny title but to me it captures the essence of midlife as I am living it now.

PABX (Private Automatic Branch Exchange)
Connecting all Departments

Did you hear me
Say good night
I said it softly
Upon a star.

I heard you
You said it softly, too
I went to bed

Starlit.

That's what I am in midlife. Starlit.

A Second Debut

Gemma Guerrero Cruz

In my adolescence, that painful episode of secret insecurities, there was a gorgeous swan who tormented me with her beauty. But the vicissitudes of her life, which I observed from a safe distance, unwittingly gave me valuable lessons on how to transform middle age from a dreaded period of decline into a happy, meaningful rebirth.

The Swan is old enough to be my mother, yet in her brilliant presence I have always felt awkward, badly dressed, and insignificant. Perhaps it is because she has always been so dazzling, though not exclusively in the physical sense, that I have always felt like an ugly duckling beside her.

She was born not only with a silver spoon in her mouth but with an almost infallible eye for color and form. A kind of Midas, she can transform the dullest chunk of matter into an object of incredible beauty. Her favorite canvas has been herself, her life. She has painted

33

various transformations of her own physical and spiritual being, sometimes with broad, abstract strokes no one understood, and at other times in impressionistic images and more recently, in realistic, colorful collages.

The first time I saw her was at Sunday lunch at my grandfather's house in Pasay. She was my uncle's fiancee and she arrived in a minute sports car, when none of us children had ever seen one. She was wearing an aqua halter dress, a wide-brimmed straw hat, matching espadrilles, looking every inch like a Hollywood film star.

According to the family grapevine, she was bred and educated in Europe and I (much later) would imagine her radiating irresistible charm from Deuville to the Bosphorus, elbowing her way through a phalanx of suitors and admirers, only to come back and marry my relative. She smirked at me indifferently that Sunday, as she caught me gaping at her, awestruck, under a *chico* tree by the driveway.

Our next encounter could not be avoided and was just as discomfiting. I was already seventeen by then. She hardly looked a year older than when I last saw her sliding out of that cute convertible at Grandfather's house. She and her husband had been away most of the time, I was informed, but were back for good, with two babies. She was taking a crack at pret-a-porter clothes with European patterns, imported fabrics, exquisite accessories like tortoise buttons, sterling silver buckles, and the sparkle of faceted jet beads. Her previous enterprises, so I heard, were an Oriental cafe behind L'Opera in Paris, the decor and the cuisine both a raging success; an upper-market curio shop at Marbella; and a lace factory in Belgium that made wedding gowns for royalty. She was always doing something, and whatever it was she touched, she turned into beauty and gold.

I needed an appropriate wardrobe as I was going to Europe, for the first time, with a group of eager schoolmates, chaperoned by two nuns. My mother sent me to her perfumed salon.

The Swan was gliding among swatches of precious silk, bolts of translucent chiffon in rainbow colors, yards of sedate Prince of Wales and glen plaid. She had shed off that copper cascade which reflected the rays of a Sunday sun and looked very Valentino-style with an

34

ebony, angular bob, so heavily gelled it looked as if it had been painted on her head. She was businesslike but effortlessly chic in a claret and grey suit: power-dressing light- years before *Vogue* gave its imprimatur to that kind of fashion statement.

I was already a head taller than she and had grown to her dress size.

"Fancy that," she exclaimed, as I was young enough to be her daughter and already had the same waistline as she.

"God, what hips you've inherited from the Cruzes." What would I look like when I got to be her age? Painful words to an adolescent from a woman who must have been close to fifty.

She took two outfits from a refurbished antique armoire and casually pulled them off their quilted satin hangers and told me to try them on. Gingerly, I sneaked into the double knit dress, afraid of snagging the luxurious fabric on a hang nail. It was crease-resistant, hand washable, perfect for doing Europe at the speed of two cities a day. A long-sleeved nothing dress at first sight, it turned out to be sheer opulence on closer inspection. That chartreuse dress was lined with the purest printed silk, a burst of autumn foliage, such precious, hedonistic details only the wearer could appreciate, or perhaps reveal in deepest intimacy. (Years later, as I strolled through my first autumn forest at Henley, it was the silk lining of that dress that suddenly flashed in my mind.)

The other outfit was ochre, like the mane of a healthy lion, with a high-necked silk collar and cuffs in a bold leopard print. But the rest of the animal was imprisoned inside, for my eyes only, like a second skin.

Certainly, the Swan did not dress only for dramatic effect; she dressed for herself first and foremost when most of her contemporaries had let themselves go. Her self-esteem bordered on sheer egoism, I thought. Much later, I realized that more than vanity, it was a manifestation of an inner rage, a perpetual silent turmoil that kept her fascinating, and fascinated with life, until she was way past sixty.

There were other garments she pulled out of the drawers of that same *aparador*: a car coat in a bulky mixed knit, a burgundy jumper, a black woolen pencil skirt that hovered above the kneecaps, and an assortment of blouses, one with bat sleeves, another with a Peter Pan collar, and still another with a boat neck. Apparently, she was also going abroad and had made all those lovely clothes for herself, but she gave them to me without even asking if I liked them.

"Enjoy them. I'll make another batch for myself," she said. "But do take care of that figure." I noticed that the smirk had mellowed into an almost motherly smile.

Then I lost track of her.

WE MET AGAIN after the dictatorship, in another country halfway around the world. By that time, I had left my husband and the Swan had been widowed. I was a guest at a conference about American intervention and she heard about this from other Filipinos, so everywhere there were messages for me to call and visit her at a new domain.

Should I? I asked myself. Definitely, I thought, even at the risk of feeling awkward, badly dressed, and insignificant, at the threshold of my own midlife. I did not need to feel like an ugly duckling again, an uncomfortable atavistic emotion which made me realize that in her presence I could never feel like a swan. As I had not heard from her nor seen her for decades, I had forgotten, so once again, like in that distant Sunday, I was overwhelmed by the manifestations of her exquisite taste. To her, it came so naturally: that congenital refinement, the irrepressible exuberance of each one of her transformations.

But, for the first time in her life, the Swan was also completely alone, except for a faithful maidservant. There were no more babies to raise, no husband to pamper, no more lovers, and gone was the phalanx of suitors and admirers from Deuville to the Bosphorus. She had her life back. Did she know what to do with it?

The living room was literally bursting with flowers: vermillion tiger lilies on an onyx coffee table, a shower of green orchids that fell from mantelpiece to carpet. (Solitude did not seem to bother the Swan.) Red wine had been decantered in a Bacarat flask, in preparation for my visit, I wanted to think. There were candles on the antique silver candelabras ready to be lit. Through the picture window, a white, flimsy tent-like structure with a lighted chandelier etched its sensuous form against the desert sunset.

Her entrance was regal but casual, not at all intimidating (perhaps because I had grown older). Her eyes were brimming with tears as she showed me photographs of ourselves, the family, I had never dreamt she would cherish. She still had slim, schoolgirl hips (mine had spread a few inches wider); she had a subtle tan (from early morning walks in the desert to alleviate an asthmatic condition). Her hair, now a dark auburn, was done up as in a Damian Domingo portrait, with wisps and subtle waves framing a past midlife counte-nance.

"No one prepares us for old age, *hija*," were her words of welcome, uttered affectionately, without a tinge of bitterness or regret. "Women are prepared to become brides, housewives and mothers.... even beauty queens...." There was a significant pause, and then, "but no one educates us to be old and alone. No one prepares us for a second debut."

She was merely stating a fact, yet I felt she had already found a solution to the minor problem and that I was about to benefit from her life's experience. This encounter was going to be an intensive course. The Swan was reclined on one of the voluptuous leather couches, like an art nouveau odalisque. She had such graceful limbs even in "old age."

There were no traces of the severe Valentino cut of her pret-a-porter days or that copper cascade that must have launched a thousand gondolas in Venice before she returned to Manila to marry my uncle. But the uniqueness of her character was there unravaged by time: the "rage to live," as I so often described it, that "inner turmoil" which had kept her vibrant and irrepressible.

Even in the privacy of her own home, there were no frayed edges on the cuffs of her lounging robe nor on her personality. She was elegant and graceful from dawn to dusk; in perfect harmony with herself and the world about her. I was happy I had mustered enough courage to see her, at the risk of being devastated by her dazzling presence. It was time to listen and to learn.

The day after, we were sipping an exotic blend of coffee at the heart of a fashionable shopping mall not far from where she lived.

"Look at that woman," the Swan suddenly said. "She is younger than I but not young enough for that hairstyle. It's wrong. It's much too drastic and severe for someone her age and for that jogging outfit she's wearing."

The person in question was sporting a kind of boy's bob, with a fluff on the forehead, very popular among matrons of a certain age (and executive level) in Manila.

"Those famous designers and beauty specialists all ignore women my age. There should be salons especially for grooming and dressing women over sixty," she declared. "Everyone wants to stay young, look young. No one wants to admit that she is getting old. That is why most women are totally unprepared for this period of life. Someone like Vidal Sassoon should do something about our physical appearance. But for the rest of you, which is more important, you have to figure that out yourself."

The lesson had begun.

"He would probably lose his clients," I said, and she agreed but insisted that at midlife a woman's hairdo should be softer, her clothes more graceful, in fabrics that flow and swirl around her knees or ankles.

She spoke in parables. Her amusing monologues on how to conceal a dowager hump, how to program cosmetic lifts so they do not look too drastic, the virtues of nonalcoholic drinks and carrot juice, of virgin olive oil as a hair conditioner, disguised precious nuggets of wisdom.

"Obviously, the most essential element is a solid economic base," she continued. "Some women inherit fortunes from either parents or spouses, but the rest of us will have to take care of our own economic future."

"No wonder you were always doing something!" I exclaimed. Even a politically stable country founders when its economic system deteriorates, so a middle-aged woman's gross personal product should at least be enough to cover her basic zoological needs. The Swan must have been subconsciously preparing for midlife in her younger years.

"It is not only the accumulation of capital, as you call it," she said. "It is more of an accumulation of skills, even day-to-day skills, the simplest ones, and your attitude to work," the Swan clarified.

At past sixty, she drives to the supermarket, loads and unloads her grocery bags, prepares elaborate meals for herself and her servant, putters around her small garden, as if she were still a young house-wife. All the heaving, weaving through traffic, parking, walking to and from one's destination, which most women her age might consider a punishment, are to her skills that should be improved and never forgotten.

"One's attitude towards work inevitably affects one's state of mind. Many women feel aggrieved that their husbands (or fathers) did not provide for them. They are sorry for themselves, they pity themselves because they have to earn a living either by being employed or by setting up a business," she said.

"Sometimes I catch myself feeling that way," I confessed.

"Perish that thought," she said, shaking her head.

Like the ancient Aztecs, the Swan regards work not as a punishment or a burden but as a vital part of life, as the fullest and most glorious expression of it.

The key is to see oneself truthfully, never to limit one's self, but to know the extent of one's endurance and capabilities. The secret is to transform one's self, continuously, without prejudice or fear.

I am applying most of Swan's time-tested theories to my own life, determined as I am to convert midlife into a second debut.

PRIVILEGE AND PAIN

NENI STA. ROMANA-CRUZ

THE DAY the optometrist so very gently told me that my compromise contact lenses would no longer do, I knew that the era of the bifocals had begun for me. When she found out I was fortyish, thus confirming all her suspicions, she broke the news like it were some dreaded disease she was poised to announce. Certainly I was not the first patient to receive a diagnosis of such gravity, but perhaps she was fearful I would end up in a fit. And since she had been there before, she knew how traumatic such confirmation of the coming of age can be.

Women older and wiser than I speak of harsher, more dramatic initiations into midlife. The first hint of greying, the worry lines that concealers can no longer remedy, the unwanted circles under the eyes that teabags and cucumbers can no longer remove, the battle with the bulge. I cannot even lay claim to such drama, for midlife came to me almost unnoticed.

It must have begun when my birthdays became days to shirk from rather than look forward to. I could not understand my sudden social ineptness in graciously acknowledging greetings and warm wishes from friends. No, it was not because I was fearful of revealing my age for people were far too polite to ask, or, having been my schoolmates, knew from yesteryear's slum books and debuts and other such milestones that we were just months apart. My idea of a birthday well spent was to withdraw completely from the world just for this day for nothing more eventful than locking myself up in the bedroom and sleeping through it all.

From probing into myself, I knew it was because birthdays had become my self-imposed period for looking back, taking stock, and asking the crucial and the critical "What do you have to show for all these years?" Or, how does one justify birthday after birthday? Those were questions no one but I ever asked but I wanted substantive answers to them nevertheless.

Adding to the seasonal anxiety would be the nagging thought: Is there time enough left to realize one's many dreams?

My friends say I am too hard on myself, for whoever said I had to be accountable for every birthday? They insist that I need to relax, enjoy the richness and contradictions of life more rather than looking for what is not there, revel in the present rather than pining for what is yet to come.

And I think they may be right, as I listen to them blissfully chatter away about concerns more immediate, more mundane. For instance, the pros and cons of a hysterectomy, as if total happiness and the fate of a marriage depended on it. But perhaps they both do.

The conversation buzzes on, following the usual familiar illogic that we are all accustomed to, revealing what is most pressing in the medley of female consciousness represented here. Genggay bears witness to an antiwrinkling cream imported from Romania, flaunting her schoolgirl glow as incontrovertible evidence. Maribel, who has made Sao Paulo her second home, swears by yet another cream, especially mailed to her at regular intervals. With characteristic humor, she says, "Of course, you will not see the results till ten years from now...." Her voice trails off, for how is she to continue what is the obvious rude other half of her statement—". . . when I shall look younger than all the rest of you?"- without being stoned? Wendy speaks of the discovery that the best organic substance for the skin comes from the thin film or tissue that infants of the mammal family are born with. Meiling, who was never known to be vain, now worries about what archcritic Rochit might say about her makeup or hairstyle or wardrobe. BeAnn, the corporate executive, religiously resorts to her color mousse, laughing off fears of chemical dyes causing brain damage and declaring that her vanity transcends all that. Linda has undertaken a strict daily walking ritual to revert to her old self of twenty or so pounds ago and now proudly bares slim arms when she wears sleeveless dresses. Diane swears by her dancing session every Tuesday night, quite fortunately with her husband and not with the sought-after, greasy-haired, nimblefooted, glib-tongued "attorneys" who charge hourly rates. Dancing is primarily for Diane's health and newfound youthful abandon. Mayen spends much of her day in tennis, jogging, Spanish dancing, working out at the gym and nibbling at health foods. Openly vain, she prefers to dissociate herself from class reunions because those are the most telling evidence of her age. Rose has recently discovered the font of all youthfulness in powdered health formulas, expensive of course, since the cost is computed on the basis of the almighty US dollar, but they are supposed to be the answer to all of our body's nutritional require- ments. She counsels everyone who cares to heed her advice on the virtues of a daily sunblock and baring one's neck to full advantage now while it is still wrinkle-free. Not all my friends are health freaks, for Jojo complains that such healthful concoctions taste like the good earth and everything else unpalatable. For her, there is nothing like those heavenly, excessive calories to accompany one's meal. And still for many others, religion and community worship have given their empty lives a richer dimension. Religious movements abound for every mood and persuasion and the plethora of acronyms can baffle. With us, it is truly to each her own high.

But it is in the intimacy of smaller groups that the more delicate issues are unburdened. How and why do marriages turn sour? Must they go awry all because one has not turned out to be the consummate cook and homemaker that his mother was? Can husband and wife be both lovers and friends? How to keep alive the romance and passion of the first date or even of forsaken first loves? How accurate is every woman's favorite role model and guru, Gilda, whose usual use of language is faultless, when she alludes to marital bliss as "as happy as one can possibly be in a marriage"?

The curious thing is that even at their most vulnerable, the troubled women never lose their gift of laughter. Daisy of the checkered life, who has remained blissfully unmarried, loves to tease the widow in her class for acquiring a second husband while she has yet to get her first. And for those who have been married over five years, the concerns take on a different twist. Is it really such a crime to have neglected the salad greens which have now turned a sickly yellow in the ref crisper, else why would it turn into a major irritant? Is it such a sin of omission not to know your spouse's shoe size after all these years? Did our mothers and other women of earlier generations also feel the need to get away from it all periodically? In their lifetime, were they also, like Shayne and company plagued with the burdens of being woman, experiencing the urge to bathe in the magical and enervating springwaters of Mt. Banahaw? And the sudden realization that since the same issues are brought up at each and every all-girls night out, we may all be destined to still be so indecisive and bewildered even at age ninety-five? Would a woman's life be considered less than complete if it could not tell of an experience as intense and momentous as the transformed heroine-housewife in *The Bridges of Madison County*?

The one thing my high school classmates and I have long agreed on is that our class fund, for which no cause seems justifiable enough for any of us, should be eventually used for the one purpose we are unanimous on-a class retirement home, in Baguio or Tagaytay or anywhere else since we will be too senile to care anyway. Our sudden mood for nostalgia and fascination with class reunions have awakened the precocious high schooler in many of us. The awakening came right in the nick of time, before we had completely turned our backs on the past, forgetting what we were like then. Since we know one another so well, we may be our own best companions in our old age. The booby prize for the class member who outlives everyone else is full entitlement to whatever remains of that disputed class fund.

We must grow old together, they cry out. But aren't we doing that already? And because the class profile is as colorful as it is, not a few have wondered if we could also create a men's wing, so that our contemporaries from Ateneo and La Salle could be accommodated as well in this reunion of reunions.

Anyone will be led to wonder how normalcy can ever occur in the lives of individuals beset with questions such as those for which there may never be satisfactory answers. But it is possible, for life does need to go on, with or without the doubts, the uncertainties, the indecisiveness.

One learns soon enough that the questions merely mirror the realities of everyday transactions and interactions. If one does not allow them to interfere or if one does not pause long enough to be rendered passive and immobile, they may just rightfully be considered metaphors for life's many intriguing complexities.

Letty is one who has come to terms with midlife. She may declare war on me forever for saying this, but most likely it is because she has had more time to experience it, confront it, come to terms with it. Although very successful in a career, she may soon leave it, both by choice and by design, as she is ready to move on to other challenges, other realms. Raised in a genteel and conservative Catholic atmosphere typical of most upper-class families, she says, addressing society: "I have played your game and abided by its rules. Now I am ready and entitled to do as I please, to do what pleases me. There is a liberating feeling knowing that."

Another individual who views retirement as simply another chapter in one's life is Ester. Having little to complain about in life except the loss of an infant daughter in childbirth, a turning point in her family life because her marriage has been blessed with only one other child, a son, she already knows that she will want to assist in the care of orphaned and abandoned children when her time comes to retire. "I have always yearned to hug a baby again and then I realized just how many babies there are in need of hugging."

Doreen may never have experienced the joys of being a physical mother, but she is no less blessed, no less fulfilled in her family, her teaching, her books, her writing, and her wealth of friends.

AND SO if birthdays terrify and the questions of self-worth never cease to nag, how have I coped? Am I coping at all?

Sometime in the past and somewhere on the long and arduous way to my being wiser and stronger and more mature, a mere three months after I got married, a serious crisis struck our family. This was something we were totally unprepared for, for our childhood was almost idyllic and unperturbed by tragedy, natural or manmade. Our parents may have been as unprepared because, for the very first time they ceased to be the pillars of strength they had always been to us their five children. It pained us to see that they were turning to us for both counsel and strength, suddenly becoming the dependent children we had always been. It was a true reversal of roles.

No one ever told me to take the lead. No one needed to. I simply assumed that as the eldest child, I had an urgent task to take on. No, I don't think I was even conscious of such a hierarchy of roles. It just happened as though it were second skin.

The shock of my brother Chito being exiled in the People's Republic of China, in those years when a trip to the moon was far easier to attain than a trip to the mainland, began to take a toll on all of us. It was a "loss" difficult to accept because it depended on the end of martial rule or the end of the Marcos era, whichever freedom from bondage came first. More difficult, perhaps, were the futile attempts to shield my parents from the "stigma" of having a son who had turned "red," if the Marcos press was to be believed at all. Why, they may not even have known the nuances of communism, aside from the godless aspect of it.

It was clear to us all that we had lost friends and even relatives who now looked at our family perhaps as having lost a degree of respectability and had earned instant notoriety. There was a price on Chito's head, he was a hunted man, the military court was hearing the subversion case with many of the accused in absentia — all these trappings of the martial law regime could not but intimidate and anger. The fourteen years of exile seemed interminable, ending only with the 1986 EDSA revolt.

Chito was finally able to return home, but home was no longer what he knew it to be. Our father and a brother had died while Chito was in exile and we had all been transformed in the process. While this chapter of a family's history may have ended quite happily, it exacted a high price from all of us, whether we would like to admit it or not.

My long-standing prayer for my mother to live long enough for Chito's homecoming was answered. She was incredulous at the dreamlike reality of it but blissful beyond compare. She was not alone, for we all felt the same way. But even that joy became shortlived, for months after, we lost our mother. Should I perhaps have added to my prayers that she be allowed to enjoy a longer time with the son she was just beginning to know all over again? I was regretting the oversight.

But it is amazing how in deep grief one must cling to whatever can provide some kind of solace, no matter how fleeting. In my seeking to make sense of this new upheaval in our lives, I rationalized that at least all four of us children were together to bid our mother a final good-bye. In the same breath, though, I had to gently remind God that this was the third death in our immediate family in twelve years. Wasn't that a little tough, a little too heavy?

The months that followed were difficult for all of us, for the absence of the anchor that our mother had been left quite a void. We missed her warmth and laughter and love for life, but we also acknowledged that she had done a wonderful job as wife and mother. And resiliency and independence are two of the many lessons she has left us.

In the context of all these, I could not but turn mindless when

47

another death in our immediate family again struck just thirteen months after, in February 1988. It happened to my only sister, Chona, the youngest member of the family — and in the most treacherous of circumstances. It is one thing to die of natural causes, but to be murdered by a killer still unknown, still on the loose?

Her story, tragic and uncanny as it is, is material that Gabriel Garcia Marquez himself could have crafted. The evil motif in her story is so pervasive it is almost palpable.

The man she married discovers her lifeless body in the dressing room, an area of the house accessible only to the couple. He is convinced that it is a suicide but all other evidence disproves the suicide theory. Guess who has surfaced as the principal suspect. This is a case of life imitating art.

The story of Chona's life and death begs to be told. But it must for the moment remain the mystery that it is because of the many existing gaps and the long, tedious legal processes it continues to be subjected to, five years later.

It must be because of the state of absurdity and mindlessness I found myself in after we lost Chona that I was never intrigued by the midlife question. It paled in urgency to my need to seek truth, peace, and justice for her.

I missed my parents as I yearned to be a child again needing refuge and protection and a sense of security. But I was glad they were gone, thus being spared this heartbreak of losing a child they had so cared for and nurtured, to a crazed assassin's bullet. How I carried on, I do not wish to remember. But I never lost my sense of duty. There was work to be done for Chona and I did not want to be found wanting. I did not question the bizarre and macabre nature of the task I had to do. I vowed to carry on because I could not help her in life. Perhaps she did not want to be helped then. I only felt sorry that I no longer had a sister and soul mate and best friend to lighten the load. It is an unspeakable loneliness that continues to carry so much pain and anguish, for even at my happiest these days I think of Chona and how much fuller these joys would be were she around to share them. It is not easy to escape one's deepest hurts, no matter how one thinks these have been tucked safely away in obscurity.

I have never found the answers to why all these have happened and I have grown weary asking questions. I sought and found much solace and consolation from a prayer of St. Francis of Sales. It is not couched in language and empty imagery that will console, but is uncomfortably blunt. Whatever cross we carry, it says, is something that Jesus Christ himself specifically fashioned for us, almost person-alized according to our capacity for pain and suffering. Its size and weight are deliberate and come to us with his own love and suffering and knowledge. Trust that it is no mere accident of fate. Need one say anything more?

In the years following Chona's death, during which those dear to me worried about the strange sadness in my eyes, I would detest being asked a polite and often innocent how-are-you because I imagined it to be nothing less than a lead to curious questions from all and sundry that I did not care to answer. And sometimes, out of exasperation and with a deliberate intent to shock, I would reply, "Very busy solving a murder!"

Impatient with the intricacies of law and the judicial process, I had said out loud that perhaps I should have been a lawyer myself. But ever since a dear lawyer-friend counseled that he or she is a fool who would try to solve his or her own legal dilemmas, I have had to quietly relearn what grace in times of great trials is all about.

Five years after, I thought I had healed. But I have merely suc-ceeded in distracting myself, in setting such cares aside. For how does one explain the same heightened anxiety I continue to go through when I receive calls from the lawyers handling Chona's case? And my persistent reluctance to visit our family home, once full of warm and pleasant memories, now recalling only irreparable losses?

Why, even the tall golden shower tree by the front gate that we all so loved because it signalled the onset of happy summers seemed to have empathized with me. It was felled by a dreadful typhoon and could not be turned upright and alive once more. The day that happened, something within me died all over again, as it was my only

49

could not be turned upright and alive once more. The day that happened, something within me died all over again, as it was my only tangible link to the persons I have loved and lost. To ease that new pain, I have had to immediately plant a young golden shower in our garden. And when it brought surprising blooms this rainy October, I did not question its being out of rhythm with the season. That signaled to me the arrival of a new summer, the beginning of a healing I so need.

THE STRANGEST of paradoxes is that despite all these, I feel truly blessed and privileged. I understand myself better and am less perplexed seeing and understanding what have contributed to the shaping of my person. After all that and having reduced all complexities to what is truly essential, I dare ask, so what else remains that could still hurt me?

Still quite a lot, it surprises me now. It is never difficult to look for sources of woe and misery. Fortunately, these are no longer issues which impinge on my sanity and my very well-being, but stuff that the educated, privileged, middle-class woman shamelessly weaves her angsts from.

But there are such good days when I feel that nothing, absolutely nothing, can mar my mood. I get a natural high from going to the wet market, sparing our cook the weekly drudgery and the required accounting. I lovingly label the fish and meats for the freezer, sectioning off areas for beef, pork, processed meat for hurried, noncreative breakfasts, chicken, fish, and tupperwares of leftovers awaiting recycling. I wax lyrical as I stir the Caesar Salad dressing with steady strokes, remembering to remain in the best of moods always lest the yolks and the olive oil refuse to cooperate. I update the freezer list and check on my four-week meal menu, precisely prepared so that the family gets respectable meals even in those long weeks when my mind is possessed by deadlines and projects having little to do with home. (Look, my mind can take only so much at any one time.) The set menu, if adhered to, and that is an altogether different story, will ensure that there are no strange way of easing my conscience for not being diligent enough about domestic concerns. It also gives me some form of control over a household system that I have grown weary of directly managing.

Oh, the pure and simple joys of an old-fashioned homemaker! My husband teases that it is because I do these so rarely (is that why my market *suki* always welcomes me back so warmly?), but even his ribbing I do not allow to spoil my sunshiny mood.

On days like these, I enjoy being home, unharried and not needing to rush off somewhere. That is when there seems to be time to see how well the grass is growing in the garden and the orchids which have learned to thrive on neglect and how long it is taking my favorite bougainvilleas to bloom again.

However, reality often sets in so rudely, when least wanted and least expected. I look at myself and realize that I am not as wonderful a homemaker as I would like to be for I would dismally fail all criteria set by those American magazines. I do not have the patience to execute my menus; I see mounds and mounds of files and useless paperwork from the past five years needing to be sorted out on top of and under my desk; the baby books of the three children, two of whom have long since left their childhood, need updating from their first birthday parties; and there are photographs waiting to be included in the family albums. Even the family library has proven useless to me because I can never locate the books I need without searching each and every shelf. Should I perhaps take a two-year sabbatical to straighten out my personal affairs? Could that be the answer to my children's subtle pleas for me to learn to relax again so that I would be less impatient with them? And the cycle begins anew for me.

That was quite an awakening the day I realized I was no longer enjoying the socials I used to love years back. In fact, it had become more disturbing for me to be invited to a function, rather than not be on any guest list. My ego had become so secure and obstinate it took much more than merely being ignored to dent it. Besides, my stamina could no longer keep up with too many of them and I was feeling I had become boring company anyway.

51

Those are times when I do not mind openly proclaiming that I have grown too old for such merrymaking and frivolities. I feel that if my presence will not be missed and will not contribute anything to the occasion, what is the sense in taking all the trouble to be there? And with very little time on my hands most of the time, I do have better things to do, thank you. The things that matter most to me, reading and writing, are such solitary activities. So it is really not just because I have turned antisocial.

I may not have completely turned my back on society's rules then if I have not been able to ignore social obligations with enough poise and élan. Not even when I reason out that life is too short for one not to care only for what one wants to do, rather than for what one is expected to do. May that self-assurance come with my complete initiation into midlife.

The troubled times I want to console myself, times when I am rational enough not to feel overwhelmed or defeated, I think of this strong woman Winnie who is intelligent, often too articulate, and happy with home and career. She is a portrait of a woman who has successfully tamed the midlife years. The most curious thing about Winnie is that she is not comfortable with the "strong" attribute pinned on her and does not at all feel complimented by it. This isn't strength, she says, for it pales in comparison to the predicament of less privileged women whose only day-to-day option is to find a way to help their husbands and their children cope with another day of poverty.

Why, these women do not even have the leisure to pause and analyze and reckon with all the things wrong in their lives, factors standing in the way of their self-actualization. And when they do, we had better be ready with answers, for we may be held accountable for the way this state of affairs is. The observation is not exaggerated or totally inaccurate that every woman who manages to find expression in a career does so at the expense of unconsciously "exploiting" another woman who must take on the mundane chores of running a home and acting as surrogate mother to the children who must have someone to come home to.

52

Within that context, one should hush and move on to matters of consequence. But it is not always easy to smile and rationalize on days when one carries the workplace's foul mood over to the home, with the very persons one values most turning out to be the unknowing, innocent victims. There have been occasions too when one's upbeat mood sours for no apparent reason. Could this just be the malaise of the educated woman, one who appears to know more than what is necessary but is really no wiser than the woman next door?

Despite my erratic mood swings, however, I am for the most part quite happy. I really should have little to complain about because my home life and career have allowed me to be myself, something I have taken quite matter-of-factly, but something that my friends have woefully told me is not always the case and I must thus consider myself singularly blessed.

Even my stint as reluctant, untrained wife to a public official and worse, electoral candidate, is something I can only now finally appreciate as a colorful chapter in my personal history. I needed saintly attributes then to accept it, for it was difficult to understand why life had drastically turned so public that the simple pleasures of family life had become part of my glowing memories. But I knew I had to keep going in fairness to a spouse who had never in the past stood in the way of my becoming, no matter how radical or unorthodox. By the same token, I had to support his own growth and dreams. His turn to be unconventional had to come sometime!

And so I continue to walk this tightrope of family, home, careers, both primary and secondary, often wondering if I'll make it and if the toll on my mental hygiene is all worthwhile. Am I doing right, I keep asking, but not pausing long enough to care to hear the answer. Is this the typical predicament of a career woman in her forties wanting to do much more than she can handle?

But I might as well come to terms with this, that even at age ninety-five, along with my friends who wonder when the time might be the most appropriate to turn their backs on their marriages, I am certain to be racked by the very same issues about being woman.

ninety-five, along with my friends who wonder when the time might be the most appropriate to turn their backs on their marriages, I am certain to be racked by the very same issues about being woman.

In the meantime, there are no regrets, no turning back. So, who's afraid of turning fifty? Here's looking right at you, those golden years which now begin to beckon.

DISABLED IN MENOPAUSE

CHIC FORTICH

I REMEMBER the first time my menses became irregular. I was jubilant! I thought I was pregnant, and my mind was filled with visions of the son I had always wanted.

I lay around for two weeks, being very careful not to move too much, practically refusing to do anything. At the end of the two-week period, I went to my gynecologist. As she gave me an internal examination, she began shaking her head.

"No, you're not pregnant," was her verdict.

I wouldn't believe her. There was that heaviness in my lower abdomen.

"I'm afraid it's menopausal," she broke the news softly.

Menopausal? "But I'm just turning thirty-nine!" I protested. "That's too young to have menopause!"

"Others start even younger," she confirmed.

When my menses still didn't come the following week, I went to see another doctor in another city. I got the same answer. I went back to my hometown, fuming mad. How dare these doctors tell me I'm growing old!

Soon after I got back home, though, my menses did come. And I plunged into a deep depression. For days, I refused to do anything but mope. In short, I disabled myself. Because I equated menopause with old age and refused to accept it, I took upon myself one handicap more than I needed.

I was born with two genetic diseases, retinitis pigmentosa and optic atrophy, both of which lead to blindness. Optic atrophy is also accompanied by deafness. When I was eighteen, my left eye was struck by a piece of wood, and from then on I have been using only my right eye.

But my diseases were diagnosed only when I was thirty-one, after an operation on my left eye did not improve its vision. Then my doctors started looking for other reasons for my failing vision and found out about the optic atrophy. They told me quite bluntly that I was going blind and deaf.

When you're given bad news while you're still feeling okay, it doesn't really bother you. So when my doctors gave me the bad news about my double disability that first time, I didn't even blink. It was my husband who shed tears of frustration because he felt so helpless.

Four years later, I had to retire from my job at a government bank because it was becoming extremely difficult for me. The following year, I went abroad, and the doctor there said the same thing that the doctors here had told me.

That sent me into a depression.

But God, in all His mercy, gives us problems He knows we can handle. He gave me a strong, resilient heart. It wasn't long before I found myself assessing what I had: I couldn't see or hear too well, but I could think. I couldn't read, but I discovered quite joyfully (after having won a Palanca award) that I could write.

That brought me out of the depression, and I began doing more and more writing, getting involved in many civic projects and proving to myself and everyone around me that my disabilities were really no big deal. I enjoyed being an "inspiration" to others.

Having thus "conquered" my disabilities, I became susceptible to the disabling depression of menopause that year when I was thirty-nine. Again, I bounced back quickly and easily. I was on the ball once more, doing a lot of things, being a "big fish in a small pond."

A few months after I turned forty, my family and I moved to Manila. There was a drastic change in life-style, a change of environment. Now I was a small fish in a big pond, a nobody.

I made a desperate attempt to rise above my anonymity by writing and producing a musical play which was praised as beautiful, but didn't do well at the tills. I tried to get a job so I could supplement my husband's income and perhaps recover a bit of my self-esteem. But nobody was hiring an overage deaf/blind woman.

By this time, I was becoming a nervous wreck and was using a Chinese medicinal oil to help me sleep. Little did I know that the medicine was destroying my skin, and before I knew what was happening, my face had turned dark grey and started growing scales. To make things even worse, I incurred a fungal infection that caused dark raised veins to develop across my face.

One day I woke up and looked in the mirror — and stepped back in horror. My eyes lay deep and dark in my swollen face that was crisscrossed by black protruding veins.

Fear gripped my heart. Was God punishing me for having turned away from Him a few months ago? Were my two months of self-imprisonment, locking myself up in my room and blaming God for everything wrong that had happened to me, now reaping their grim harvest?

My daughter rushed me to a dermatologist, who immediately put me on steroids to fight the severe infection. The swelling subsided but not enough to keep my husband, when he came home that night and entered our room, from going into shock. "What happened to you?!"

I broke down in a fit of anguished crying.

Oozing love from every pore of his body, my husband took me in his arms and held me until the tears stopped coming and my shoulders stopped heaving.

Looking back now, I realize that during those months of severe depression, I was blind in more ways than one. And the nonphysical blindness was the darker one. The physiological and psychological traumas that came with the onslaught of menopause made me see only the darkness of depression. I couldn't tackle being deaf-blind, a nobody, ugly, and growing old at the same time.

It made me blind to the love that my husband and my two daughters tried to make me feel during that period of darkness. I felt quite ugly, and that's when they would kiss and hug me more. I felt useless, and that's when they appreciated everything I did, even my "handicapped" cooking.

We began to pray together. Only then did the light begin to seep through my self-imposed darkness.

Following an urge I did not fully understand but felt quite right about, I began writing all the people I could think of, asking for forgiveness if I had hurt them, or forgiving them if they had hurt me.

Not long afterward, I began receiving offers of writing jobs. At last, I was no longer useless.

When I was forty-four, I had another false pregnancy. It lasted for months. I went from one gynecologist to another, not believing reports of "pseudosiasis" or the negative results of the ultrasound test. I hinged everything on the positive results of an early pregnancy test.

My tummy started growing. My breasts ached once in a while. I felt a twitching in my lower abdomen. I had all the symptoms of pregnancy. So why should I believe those stupid doctors who couldn't hear a fetal heartbeat when they put their stethoscopes to my stomach?

I was pregnant, and it was going to be a boy. That was that!

Then, in my "eighth month," I felt blood trickling down my thigh. I was going to miscarry!

There was nobody else at home except my houseboy, and I had him take me to the hospital.

The gynecologist put me on her examination table, looked at my blood, and told me it was just menstruation. By this time, I had already gone spiritual and was praying more often. Still, the jolt was hard.

I prayed to the Blessed Mother and asked permission to take up smoking again. For three days, I sat at my typewriter, working and smoking almost nonstop.

On the third day, a new friend, the doctor who had introduced me to the gynecologist I had just seen, fetched me from my home and took me to a chapel in Marulas, Valenzuela, Bulacan, to attend First Friday Mass. It was September 8, the birthday of the Blessed Mother. Still depressed, I decided to offer what had just happened to me as my gift to her.

I did not know it then, but that act signaled the beginning of my salvation from the disablement of my menopausal state. Because soon after that, I finally accepted the truth that I was in menopause. I had stopped being deaf and blind to what my body was telling me.

WOMEN with physical disabilities are not spared the anguish of menopause. In fact, menopause can become an additional disability for a while, unless and until something positive happens to make them realize that they have become even more disabled by it.

But perhaps their physical disabilities and their ability to transcend these make them more capable of transcending the disablements of menopause. And since this kind of gumption is not easily found in women without physical disabilities, the latter often have greater difficulty coping with problems that come with menopause.

Take the case of Dennie. She was in her early forties when her husband, a business executive, became blind after a car accident. All through their marriage, Dennie had been dependent on him. Although she herself had worked in a bank before they married, she gave up the job and became a "plain housewife" as soon as the children started coming. In effect, she lost part of her own identity and chose to become part of her husband instead. She dressed the way he expected her to, shared his friends, threw herself into being a mother, and followed his orders.

Then he became blind—and had to depend on her. The husband she had placed on a pedestal now lay in bed most of the time, refusing to move, refusing to relate, and almost entirely dependent on her.

In Dennie's eyes, he toppled off his pedestal.

She described to me how dependent on her he has become. "Soon after he wakes up in the morning, I take him to the bathroom. I stay there with him, reading him the newspapers while he does his ablutions." From the bathroom, it's back to bed for him, or maybe out to the living room or the lawn. Dennie has to stay close by, always at his beck and call.

There are no visitors, no phone calls, not even from his siblings abroad.

Dennie has time to get out of the house only when her husband doesn't need her. That's when she goes to a psychiatrist.

Her husband receives a sizable pension from his company, so he brags to her that he still supports his family even if he's blind. When she mentioned this to me, I began to suspect something.

"Dennie," I asked her, "when he became blind, did your opinion of him change?"

She paused for a few seconds before she nodded.

"Has his blindness affected your sexual relationship?" I pushed on.

Again, she nodded.

"No wonder he feels he has to keep proving his superiority," I told her. "You should know that even if you don't say anything, he can *feel* what you think of him."

Tears began to fill Dennie's eyes. She related how nasty and mean he has become, how she has to be constantly conscious of his moods and whims.

"The psychiatrist told me," she confided, "that I'm actually suffering more than he is."

But of course! And her being in her menopausal years isn't making things easier for her. For now, when she most needs to be appreciated, to be assured of his love, to be told that she's still pretty, her husband is blind and dependent on her. He is saddling her with all his resentment and anger, thus making the burden of her menopausal insecurities even heavier.

These days, Dennie's trips to the psychiatrist are more for herself than for her husband. She has become blind in her own way.

MAGGIE'S marital problems began well before the car accident that made her blind when she was forty. She was still in her early thirties when she had a hysterectomy. At the time, she was still very much the highly paid, go-getter advertising executive, and was too busy to be bothered by menopausal symptoms. Aside from her job, she was in great demand as a talent for television commercials.

As the years wore on, her earnings eclipsed those of her husband and although she would never admit it, she began to feel superior to him. Quite predictably, her husband began compensating for his insecurities by philandering.

She knew he was fooling around, but she did not allow that knowledge to affect her in any way, except to make her feel cold and aloof. Then tragedy struck. She lost her eyesight.

A series of more than ten operations followed. All throughout the ordeal, she reached out to her children, but remained cold to her husband. When the last operation still brought no hope, depression set in on her.

Blind, perhaps jobless, entering her middle years, and with a philandering husband, Maggie became even more cold and bitter. One day, alone with her husband, she told him, "You're free. You can go and leave me."

"At that time," she recalled, "all I could think of was, 'If he could play around when I was still very active, how much more now when I am blind and getting old?'"

But he stayed. "And the kids told me that they saw him cry," she added.

Maggie couldn't get her old job back anymore, but she continued to receive offers to voice commercials. That meant she still had her own income even after she became blind.

But now her husband's earnings were bigger, and she had to learn to live on a smaller budget. In a few years, the offers petered out, and the only thing left to her was a stint as a radio announcer at a Christian station.

"I found the Lord," she said. "That was how I was able to accept my state."

Today, at fifty-two, Maggie is a fulltime housewife quite content with herself.

"I didn't have any of those hot and cold flashes others talk about," she told me. "The Lord has really helped me."

And she continues to pray for her husband.

MULTIPLE sclerosis is a disease of the nerves. The pain it brings to a patient can be literally crippling.

"I live in constant pain," said Dora of her disease. "But if I don't feel pain, I begin to worry."

When she no longer feels pain in a certain area of her body, that could mean the nerves in that area have become dead.

"Sometimes I look down at my feet and see that I have been injured, but did not know it because I did not feel the pain."

Both of Dora's legs have become desensitized and are smaller than they used to be. She can no longer walk on them and so has to use a wheelchair. At home, she hobbles around on crutches, swinging her legs so she can step forward or backward.

M S is an unpredictable disease. When you're in remission, you can move around on crutches, as Dora does, or with a cane. But when an attack comes on, you go all limp and collapse in a heap on the floor, much like a rag doll.

When Dora is out of the house, she uses a wheelchair. That way, if an attack should come when she's outdoors, she just collapses in her chair rather than on the ground.

Dora had a hysterectomy in her early thirties, soon after the onset of M S, but she was too preoccupied with work that the thought of menopause never occurred to her.

Then, when she was in her early forties, her attacks became more frequent and more severe. "You know," she said as we talked about menopause, "it just occurred to me now that those attacks could have been triggered by menopause."

That is quite likely. Many people believe that multiple sclerosis, being a disease of the nerves, is caused by tension and pressure. Since menopause is accompanied by hypertension, it is easy to understand why women sclerotics usually suffer more during that period.

Doctors prescribe corticosteroids to help sclerotics cope with their disease, but patients must also be prepared for damaging side effects. Dora takes a maintenance dose of steroids, and their side effects on her have been quite adverse. The most irritating, to say the least, are the tiny inflammations, stomatitis, that have cropped up in all openings of her body — mouth, nostrils, ears, even sexual organs.

These sores were the reason for the biggest problem she and her husband had to tackle, because they put an end to their sexual relationship.

"It was a bigger problem for my husband than for me, of course," Dora recalled, "but we had a long talk about it, and he soon got over it."

She is, understandably, hyperactive. The steroids give her a lot of energy which keeps her going in her work as the head of a national organization for the handicapped. The work, Dora said, keeps her mind off herself, and so she has never experienced any of the hot flashes and other symptoms associated with menopause.

"WHAT MAKES Lorie run?" The question comes to mind as soon as one finds out how full and hectic Lorie's days are.

She was forty-three and five months pregnant when she had her first attack of multiple sclerosis.

"First, there was this pain in my foot. Then it began to go up my legs to my hips. It was so excruciating, only I could bear it," Lorie said of that first attack.

At the hospital, the doctors bombarded her with morphine. They explained that they had to do all they could to save her, even though they ran the risk of hurting the baby with the painkillers.

Two weeks later, the pain disappeared. Thinking she was well, Lorie asked her maid to help her get out of bed so she could go to the bathroom. When she stood up, she suddenly fell to the floor like a half-filled sack of potatoes. Then she realized that she couldn't feel anything in her legs anymore. She had become paralyzed.

"I never cried so much in my life," she confessed.

Her family decided that she should go to the United States. If her pregnancy was to come to full term, then it should be in a place where all possible safeguards could be taken.

When Lorie's baby was due, her doctors told her they would have to do a Caesarean section since she was paralyzed from the breast down. "I just prayed for one minute after they told me that," she said triumphantly, "and then I knew I was going into labor, even if I didn't feel anything."

She called the nurse, who wouldn't believe her when she said she was going into labor. "That's impossible!" the nurse exclaimed. But she looked and true enough, the baby was ready to come down the birth canal.

Lorie was rushed to the operating room and told to just think that she was pushing down. She did, and before long her youngest son was born.

Soon after she gave birth, she began to feel the hot flashes symptomatic of menopause. Then her menses became irregular. For three years, she suffered flashes and excessive bleeding whenever her period came.

"But when my menses would last for about ten days at a time, and I was big as a balloon, I went to the hospital. As soon as the doctor examined me, he told me to check in right away."

When Lorie came out of the operating room, a nurse told her that the doctors had removed a five-kilo tumor from her uterus, and they had to do a complete hysterectomy.

After that surgery, more of her problems were caused by the steroids the doctors had prescribed for her multiple sclerosis. Finally, after she required an operation because the steroids had eaten into her hipbone, she decided to stop taking them.

"I will bear the pain," she resolved.

And so she has. It has been years since she took her last dose of hydrocortisones, and she is managing her disease quite well.

"I have to go out every day," she explained. "If I stay home, I'll go crazy with pain."

So Lorie drives her car from one meeting to another, from one project to the next. She insists on driving because it makes her put her legs to good use. Once outside the car, she shifts from cane to crutches to wheelchair, depending on the severity of her condition.

"I still get those hot flashes," she admitted, but they don't bother her anymore.

"The doctors told my husband he should let me shout or lose my temper once in a while," she explained. "MS is caused by pressure. I used to be the long-suffering kind, keeping everything within myself. Now I've learned to shout and get mad just to let off steam.

THE STORIES of these four women and my own experience have given me more insights into the female nemesis that is menopause.

The most significant lesson is that menopause is far more than just a physiological or psychological phenomenon. It is truly and in many senses midlife, a turning point, a time when a whole compendium of forces pushes you to either a crest or a trough, depending on which way the wave of your life has been going, or where you will it to go.

In my own case, and in the cases of Maggie, Dora, and Lorie, disability either worsened or came on at the same time that menopause began. And even for Dennie, who was not the one involved in a car accident, menopause came like a disability. But only because she wanted it to be.

Let us reflect on each of these stories.

Maggie was the high-powered advertising executive. Her success, however, was actually wreaking havoc on her relationship with her husband and perhaps taking her away from her children.

Then, when menopause set in, so did disability.

The heightened emotionality of menopause made Maggie bitter about everything and even colder towards her husband. Then, as she put it, she found the Lord and her bitterness was removed. And because her husband chose to stay, her coldness towards him thawed too.

Still, she tried to cling to the vestiges of success — doing commercials, going on radio. Until the offers stopped coming. She found herself entirely dependent on her husband's earnings. It was Lesson No. 1 in the course on humility.

Maggie had to stay at home, and because she could no longer afford to hire maids, she began to do the housework herself. The top executive became a plain homemaker. Lesson No. 2.

She claims to be much happier now. She enjoys doing the housework with her children. She has more time for herself and her friends. And she feels fulfilled each time she goes out with a group to do ministry.

Despite her disability, or perhaps because of it, the turbulent waves of midlife have become, for Maggie, placid waters settling into a smooth, gentle flow.

Dora's wave was still cresting when menopause and disability came at the same time. Instead of allowing herself to be swamped by despair, she willed her life to crest even higher and herself to do even more, achieve greater success. In the process, however, she has become dependent on medication that is ravaging her body.

I hope to God Dora realizes that she must prepare herself for the day when her candle will burn out. She has to slow down and stop taking these steroids which are giving her only artificial energy and destroying her. There is no running away from disability or menopause. Running away will only make her more crippled because she is not actually conquering her disease, but only masking it with medication. Neither is she really skipping menopause. On the contrary, it is aggravating her disease.

Lorie is the typical latebloomer. Not that she wasn't achieving anything before, but she was too reticent, too timid, to let her true feelings show. By her own admission, those qualities partly triggered her multiple sclerosis.

In short, she was rather limp before a disease came that made her go all limp. Only then did she show she was made of stronger stuff.

The physiological and psychological changes that come with menopause made her susceptible to multiple sclerosis. But instead of allowing herself to be crippled by it, she used her disability, during her menopausal years, to break out of her shell and come out into the world fighting.

Of course, there was her spirituality. From the time of the miracle on the delivery table in that American hospital, Lorie's spirit grew by leaps and bounds. That spirit spurred her metamorphosis from shy girl to achiever who has conquered pain and disability.

These days she is thinking of giving seminars for "wives who want to make their husbands happy."

In my own case, midlife was more of a family affair than anything else. The crises came at the same time: a change of life-style, dislocation, my daughters' teen troubles, financial straits, the worsening of my blindness and deafness, and my menopause.

Many times through those seven years after I turned forty and began a new life in a new place, I thought our family would break up.

We had alternate fits of running away. My husband threatened to pack up and leave, I gave warnings that I was ready to go, and our daughters ran away for a few days.

I usually bore the brunt of the blame because I was wont to be erratic, and they couldn't understand me. We had shouting bouts, doors banged, fits of hysterical crying. But in between were always the hugs and the kisses and the resolve to go through everything together.

And the praying. That was what really kept us together.

Truly, a family that prays together stays together — through all the crises of midlife, and the rest of life itself.

But what about Dennie?

Sad to say, the only one in this group who does not have a physical disability is the one who has allowed menopause to become a disability.

Why? Because the wave on which she had been riding high was that of her husband, not her own. By being too dependent on him, by existing only as an extension of him, she had not bothered to make her own wave of life. Instead, she was like a paper boat rocking precariously on the high crest of his wave. When his wave suddenly broke, she got flooded out.

Still, Dennie continues to look outside of herself for reasons. Blind to her own true self, she resents her husband for having become blind. She does not realize that the real reason her husband has great difficulty getting over the trauma of sudden blindness is that she is having great difficulty getting over the various traumas of menopause. Thus, she shares his disability because she has allowed her menopausal insecurities to blind her.

No, menopause does not have to become a disability. Unless you allow it to be. But how can we prevent it from becoming one?

In much the same way one can cope with physical disability, I suppose. With courage, strength, a light heart, and a lot of faith. And love, of course. From everyone around you.

You can get that by loving yourself first, then spreading love around yourself.

That way, a beautiful life *can* begin at forty.

ONE WITH THE
UNIVERSE

MARIEL N. FRANCISCO

I WAS at a party for my yoga teacher when I saw Eddie, whom I knew from way back. In fact, I was sure he had been infatuated with me once upon a time, but as we strained to recall those long-lost days I realized he didn't remember or didn't care to. Well, I couldn't blame him for being somewhat befuddled; he had just blown back into town after ending his fifteen-year marriage, he confided, and was trying to get his life back on track—this time, his way.

"So, let's drink to that !" I tried to cheer him up, leading the way to the wine table.

"Uh, no, thanks. I'm breaking my fast." He patted his thin tummy. My eyes lit up.

"What fast?" I asked with bated breath.

"I go on this cleansing diet now and then," he started, afraid to bore me by saying more. But I waited. "I take only carrot juice and

69

alfalfa tablets for a week to detoxify my system." He was sure he had lost me.

"You mean you've got a clean colon too?" I gasped. Had I really found a man after my own heart?

"Of course! I do a coffee enema twice a day," he bragged, as I knew he had every right to.

"Ah... where do you get your psyllium and bentonite?" I lowered my voice conspiratorially. And we broke up laughing and gave each other "fayb."

YES, A MALADY afflicts many of us as we enter midlife. We see all the parts of ourselves that we had neglected all these years and we want to correct the imbalance—right now!—before old age, illness, or death strikes us down. New choices, tantalizing possibilities, are suddenly open to us; we want to be healthy, sexy, and enlightened all at the same time. We verge on the ridiculous, provoking a crisis. And when that happens, all we can do is to affirm ourselves with a mega-dose of the endorphins produced by hearty, gut-filling laughter.

Actually, it's not so funny. It is a wrenching, soulful process, after which no man or woman is the same again. It usually attacks those between the ages of thirty-five and forty-two, but for the very repressed, distracted or retarded, it may manifest itself late, between forty-two and forty-nine. (Like the other stages of human development, it comes in seven-year periods.) It is a time of transition, so something is ending, but something is also vibrantly beginning.

What signals its onset is often an event that seems external enough, such as getting a promotion, or finding a lump in one's breast, or discovering that one's accountant has run off with the year's profits. But upon closer examination, it becomes clear that an internal process had started long before that. In fact, scientists as well as metaphysical thinkers say this is such an orderly universe nothing is ever "just an accident." At each point in our lives we attract the experiences we need to learn the lessons which will help us evolve to the next stage. Pain is a symptom of disharmony, and when we hurt enough, we change—at first in miniscule ways, then more and more momentously.

As colons are cleansed, pantries are decaffeinated, and closets un-clogged, jobs, friends, mates, gods, and sometimes even life itself, may be chucked.

At forty-four, my friend Eddie just knew he couldn't take one more day of his job as a computer executive in Honolulu. He had been a nonconformist in college, and he couldn't believe he had spent fifteen years going after this ranch-style house and two-car garage just like every Tom, Dick, and Harry. He wanted to go back to Manila and do something that would make a difference in people's lives. But his wife had found her well-paying niche in the State Department, and no way was she going to give it up. They thought breaking up was hard enough to do, until they got to the bottom line: their set of Black and Decker power tools. He assumed they were his, but she insisted they were hers, and after hard and hostile negotiation, she got the sander and he got the saw. You'd think they'd both get the message—what good is one without the other?—but by then too many hurting words had been said and there was no turning back.

Another friend of mine delivered her last baby and had her hys-terectomy and discovered her husband's affair, all as she turned thirty-nine. She got so fed up with all her friends' endless reporting of her husband's shenanigans to her, she changed them all. Her new set of friends knew nothing and she found peace at last. She discovered her talent for flower-making and started a fulfilling and profitable busi-ness, and when her husband repented, she had to think very hard whether she wanted him back or not.

I DID NOT SUSPECT there was more to it than just my carelessness when I met my "accident" within the first hour of the first stop of a projected month-long tour of China. Woozy after a bumpy flight from Hongkong to Kunming, I fell from a concrete platform and fractured my foot. Herbal decoctions brought down the swelling and eased the pain, but after a week of shopping and sightseeing piggy-back on our hefty Chinese guide, I had to be shipped back to Manila in a wheelchair.

My fracture kept me housebound for a month, proving that the office could run very well without me. To add insult to injury, my doctor remarked half-jokingly that had I been ten pounds lighter and ten years younger I would have withstood the fall better. Ouch! Ouch! I was aging, overweight, and disabled. What else could go wrong?

Plenty.

Life is indeed full of irony. Very often, a period of great external success is also a period of deep trauma, though at first it goes unnoticed. Three years earlier, after ten years at what we teachers good-naturedly refer to as "charity work," I had received a generous Fulbright grant for further professional training in the US. Upon my return, I had been tapped for a new university project with an international organization and for the first time in my life I had the petty satisfaction of knowing that I was earning more than my husband's secretary. I had just turned forty, and in more ways than I realized, my life was beginning.

The demands of the job, especially after I was promoted to director of the program, triggered many inner conflicts. In short, I wasn't sure if it was where I really wanted to be at that point in my life. The fact that I was devoting my skills and energies to foreigners and that I was under the supervision of two Americans especially grated on my hard-earned nationalist consciousness. I felt just like the Philippines wanting to grow out of the special ward status imposed by the RP-US Military Bases Agreement.

The long drive to our cramped downtown offices, rigid working hours, and bureaucratic atmosphere also oppressed me. I missed the intellectual talk in the college cafeteria and the cool acacia trees of the campus. More and more the rounds of socials and travel required by my job took time away from my family life. I was often tense and moody. There was the thrill of seeing our dreams come true in a house we were building in a beautiful spot in the suburbs, but C. and I were spending less and less time in togetherness. Unyielding, the achiever in me plodded on and imposed the highest standards of performance on myself and my staff. I did not even allow myself to grieve over a tragic incident that had happened a few months back.

We were on Christmas break when two of the Korean fellows (young professionals in the Korean health ministry) participating in our program ventured on their own to Mount Mayon. Outside Tabaco, Albay, they were accosted by bandits claiming to be with the NPA, robbed of their valuables, and fired upon. The man suffered two bullet wounds but survived; the woman was killed. It was New Year's Eve, 1988. I see myself in my darkened office, searching the files with trembling hands for our foreign charges' home telephone numbers so we could inform their families. I hear the sound of alarmed, anguished voices on the other end of the line, and I cringe and curse my country for its cruel inhospitality.

Many sleepless hours later, at the funeral parlor, I awaited the arrival of the body from Legaspi and accompanied it to the morgue to make the official identification. Oh, Miss Kim! How lovely and lily-white you looked, not a blemish on your pale skin except where the eight blasts of the homemade pistol had almost ripped off your ear. I arranged your hair as I knew you would have wanted it, and adorned your neck with a pink scarf to match the dab of color on your lips. Everyone marveled at how composed I was. And when your mother came and crumpled to the floor at the sight of your coffin, even as I caught her I must have willed my heart to stop beating, for no tears came.

The summer holiday in China with C. and Nini, our eldest daughter, was supposed to be a much needed "break"—and so it was, literally. Hobbling about on crutches, I was forced to reflect that perhaps this was life's way of telling me to slow down and be quiet. It was the start of a long depression. Although the rest of the year brought many professional achievements, I felt no glory.

We had moved into our new home, but trying to get organized only brought me more stress. For the first time in our eighteen-year marriage, our sex life was so joyless C. and I began to suspect wrong *feng-shui*: perhaps our bed should face northwest instead of southeast? An originally mild congenital heart condition started giving me pain and required medication. In August, I bled heavily and cysts of operable size were discovered in my ovaries. As my term with the project ended, the prospect of a total hysterectomy loomed. I decided to take a year off to reclaim my life.

And in the freedom of that bit of time and space, I discovered the New Age.

I had no idea then that there was such a thing. I simply found myself resonating with many happily discovered truths without realizing it was because they were all answering my need for balance and wholeness. To some people, New Age thought is either patently evil or essentially harmless, but to me it says many positive things. I think of it not as an organized movement with a specific goal, but as an attitude—a universal convergence of consciousness which suffuses all that gives meaning and purpose to our postmodern world.

It is an attitude of openness to possibilities, of trust and hope in the human spirit, of belief in evolution and progress. It is struggling peacefully, creatively resolving conflict, and seeing that everything is part of a coherent whole. It is finding answers to life's big and small mysteries, knowing that we always have a choice. It is being responsible for ourselves and knowing that we can change only ourselves, and when we change the world will change, but when we are stuck we hold back the whole of humanity—nay, the whole of creation.

New Age thought is not really new. True, it was triggered by extraordinary leaps in science at the beginning of this century which have revised the way we look at the world, but it is also ancient wisdom. It is "a complex, multidimensional crisis whose facets touch every aspect of our lives," says Berkeley physicist Fritjof Capra in *The Turning Point* (1982), "... a transition of planetary dimensions."

The New Age is *detente* and *glasnost* and *perestroika*. It is the Berlin Wall tumbling and US bases scramming. It is the NDF and RAM peace-talking, and people self-empowering. It is the greenies, ecology, and organic farming; *pito-pito* tea cocktail partying; tribal culture ballet-ing. It is the Chinese waltzing and the Russians ohm-ing; Buddhists and Christians kissing; science and theology meeting. It is win-win thinking, whole-brains intuiting, male and female soul mating.

So what have my ovarian cysts got to do with these cosmic events? Simple. They are part of a naturally evolving universe which has been programmed for growth. It was time for me to grow, but I couldn't (at least, not in the ways I wanted to), so my ovaries grew for me! The cysts were my body's reaction to the messages of distress I was sending.

Thus intimated Beth M., a lovely naturopath, who first gave me an inkling that my physical condition was the outward manifestation of my inner state. Her equally lovely sister, Evelyn A., a diet counselor and iridologist, introduced me to the idea of proper food combining which prevents toxins from building up in the body, and prescribed herbal supplements to strengthen my reproductive organs. At first I thought I would die on the fish-and-vegetable diet they put me on. But as I began to lose weight and feel better, I crossed pork and beef off my monthly grocery list. Talk to your body, they urged me. Our millions of cells are so intelligent they do their work without our even knowing it; imagine what they could do at our conscious bidding!

Next, I had to learn to un-stress myself, so Beth enrolled me in a Core Energy seminar. Now, this was going a bit far, I felt. Having been in the teaching profession for years, I looked askance at anyone claiming to teach anything outside the hallowed halls of academe. Hmmph! A commercialized, amateurish attempt, I was willing to bet. And sure enough, I was unimpressed by the quiet, laid-back style of Maraya C., the facilitator. I thought only a powerful leader-type lecturer could convince people to change. I didn't care to take my shoes off and sit on the floor with this motley roomful of strangers. In fact, I wasn't even sure I wanted to be there.

But I listened when they started sharing the details of their personal lives that had brought them there—a drug addict brother here, an abusive father there, an emotionally dependent mother here, a gambler-swindler husband there. I was surprised at everybody's openness. No one even talked of what he or she did in the outside world; all of them were just their bare selves. I was sympathetic, but I blamed them for not running their lives better.

In a detached way, I did the nine-joint exercises for relaxation. To my dismay, I was so stiff I couldn't even do the pelvic roll. ("But aren't you married?" Maraya asked, puzzled.) I also had trouble getting anything out of the meditation. It was the first time I had ever sat quietly trying not to think and I just couldn't see what use it was. When Maraya told us to lie down on the floor in fetal position, thrash about and release old hurts, frankly I couldn't think of any. But when we were massaging each other's backs, my partner touched an achy spot I wasn't even aware of. And when Maraya came to soothe away the blocked emotions with wise and gentle fingers, I couldn't believe how someone who didn't know you, could care enough to touch you so lovingly. And perhaps a little window in my heart opened.

One exercise that Maraya had us do struck me especially. Picture your life as a flower of many petals, she said, with your "I" in the center. The petals are your roles—wife, mother, career woman, daughter, sister, friend, etc. Now, tear off each petal one by one, and what have you got? "Nothing," I said without a moment's hesitation. If I was not anybody's wife and mother and teacher and daughter and sister, then what was I? What else was left? "There's you, the 'I' in the center," Maraya said. "The constant in all those roles. If you are fully present in whatever you do, there is no conflict."

I didn't fully understand what that meant, but I sensed its relevance to me. I knew what made me most unhappy was feeling fragmented by my multiple roles. In the middle of a party, I would feel guilty for enjoying myself instead of being home with C. and the children. When domestic chores required my attention, I had angry outbursts and scolded everybody for expecting me to do everything. My friend Cynthia L. and I were always needing excuses to explain our modest achievements compared with those of some colleagues: "She has no convictions," or "He has a wife," or "He's a priest." We felt so burnt-out pushing ourselves to do everything well and knowing it was all haphazard. These are the trade-offs a woman today has to make, we philosophized. But one part of us felt triumphant, while another part felt trapped.

SO MY SEARCH for health became a search for self. I realized that one goes through an identity crisis all over again at midlife, as one did in adolescence. Just when we have the different compartments of our lives down pat, we find they need to connect. We have put all our energies into pursuing certain goals and ideals, but when we get there, we ask, is this really what I want to do with my life? Has it been worth it? Are these my values, or have I naively gone along with my parents, church, school, tribe, spouse, corporation? What do I really believe in?

Who am I?

As soon as you decide what you want, New Agers believe, the universe will conspire to bring about its fruition. (If you don't know what you want, how will you get it?) In the language of the Bible, seek and you shall find. As this became a living question in me, paths to self-knowledge appeared from out of nowhere. A friend I had lost touch with suddenly invited me to an Enneagram Workshop. This, I learned, is a tool for understanding one's personality type and direction of growth based on ancient mystical knowledge (which, interestingly enough, jibes with Jungian psychology). I was so out of touch with myself that at the end of the three days I still could not pinpoint which of nine personality types I most identified with. I was confused and disappointed. I criticized myself for being a bundle of contradictions. Still, I felt I made progress in opening myself up to a group, in accepting others without judgment, and in being able to laugh, cry, and pray with them. With our facilitator Brother John's childlike joyfulness in song, body prayer, meditation, and creative ritual, I was even warming up a bit to becoming a real Catholic again.

"When the student is ready, the master will come" is another cliché thrown about by New Agers, totally taken for granted in the way only profound truths can be. Of course, in my world it was always the students who went to the teacher; this reverse idea really fascinated me because it was exactly what was happening to me. Once I decided to become a student, to learn what I could apply to my life and not just accumulate more knowledge, teachers started coming my way one by one.

What else but the most indulgent forces of the universe could have washed Gilda and me onto the doorstep of Nicky P., who we never knew existed right in our part of town? We drifted into study sessions led by this serious young philosopher, visionary, and environmental activist (who has never forgiven me for including his lofty causes and convictions in my New Age grab-bag) and relearned the most basic, most valuable, lesson of all: paying attention.

Indeed, as the recent best-seller reminds us, "All I need to know, I learned in kindergarten," but we forgot it somewhere along the way to graduate school. Pay attention. Awareness is all. Be mindful. This is nothing new; it is also what Buddhism and other meditative traditions teach. Live in the present moment. Whether playing with a child, talking with a friend, stirring the stew, taking a walk, listening to wind chimes, or making love, it is only when we pay attention, when we are present in body, mind, and spirit, that we are fully human and fully free.

Something clicked into place. I recognized this to be the same idea that Maraya had expressed about bringing the "I" into everything we do. It made more and more sense as I listened on.

This is what "presence of mind" really means, said Georg Kuhlewind, the German-Hungarian philosopher of consciousness and brilliant author of our study text, *From Normal to Healthy* (1988), who came to Manila on Nicky's invitation to give us a special workshop. In concentration exercises he showed us that we spend our lives being un-free, not even in control of our thinking processes, or knowing where our thoughts come from. (Parents? Society? Ten Commandments?) Someone who has "presence of mind" is always able to do creatively and without compulsion exactly what the situation calls for, not needing to stop and "think." This goes beyond the mere rationality developed by our Westernized education. It implies a highly developed power of insight and intuition which allows us to touch the divine source of our freedom.

The way to fight for our freedom, Kuhlewind said, is by willing ourselves to pay attention to our thinking processes. The path of knowledge really begins with one simple (but not easy) step: dissolving one bad habit, breaking one pattern of behavior, dropping the ego. These are all preliminary to meditation, wherein we become one with an experience through intense attentiveness. For a start, we did simple exercises for ten minutes a day, like listening to someone without judging or interrupting, or speaking only when we had something constructive to say, or reviewing the events of the day backwards. Only human beings, Kuhlewind concluded, have this capacity to keep making a new beginning.

Impatient to begin, Gilda and I tried doing meditation on our own, but it soon became obvious that we needed a teacher. Sure enough, we unexpectedly encountered Lito M. at a Christmas-left-overs party at Odette's. I had not seen him since our university days, when he was a cute but maladjusted kid just out of the seminary. Now his hair was all white and he seemed more at peace with himself. When he offered to conduct a series of meditation sessions for us, how little we suspected its power to change us and our lives.

Before we could benefit from meditation, Lito explained, we had to go through a process of catharsis, to become-aware and get rid of mental and emotional baggage cluttering our souls. He guided our group in the basics of relaxing with our breath, getting in touch with our innermost self, staying in that quiet place, and listening to the still, small voice inside us. Out tumbled memories and obsessions which we had long pushed down into the subconscious. Rosa recalled her mother's oppression by her in-laws and suddenly understood her own compulsive feelings for the underdog. Gilda was a lonely little girl again, fondling beloved bric-a-brac on top of her mother's dresser. Arline saw a wolf with sharp fangs peering into the window of her childhood home; it opened its mouth and just as it swallowed her she caught a glimpse of her mother looking at her. (As for those who snored away, well, they weren't ready, that's all.)

I experienced this in one of our rose meditations:

> *I saw myself as a bright red rose, fully blown, the petals so firm and open one could see the delicate yellow center. I was growing in what I recognized to be my own garden, swaying softly in the wind, green grass and trees all around me. My eyes were closed*

79

and I was smiling in serene contentment, just soaking in all the pleasant sensations of being warmed by the morning sunshine and cooled by a gentle breeze. I felt totally in harmony with everything, thinking nothing, desiring nothing. I felt I was meant to be there forever.

Then a voice asked: "What are you doing?" And I answered nonchalantly: "Nothing, I'm just being," and I smiled on. Another voice came along, and another, and another, and all asked: "What are you doing?" Again I said: "Nothing, I'm just being...myself," still smiling happily. Then everyone left me alone, and I loved being by myself, and smiling.

I felt I was sweeping all the cobwebs from my very being. I saw very clearly that I was meant to be just me, and learning to accept myself was the key to inner harmony. I had been feeling negative about myself, rejecting all the qualities I associated with my teacher self-image, when I simply had to acknowledge they were me, too. What I saw as contradictions, I realized, were just changing expressions of myself. From then on, sporadic insights began to shape a long list of the polarities I needed to embrace to achieve wholeness:

judgmental/ open
critical/ loving
self-conscious/ spontaneous
rigid/ creative
habitual/ intuitive
structured/ flowing
reasoning/ feeling
conventional/ innovative
competent/ wise
serious/ joyful
working/ helping
fragmented/ integrated

And lo, another teacher and model came who embodied this ideal. Friedemann S., a doctor of philosophy educated in Germany, England, and the US, impressed our study group with his wide and intense scholarship, but above all, his warm humanity. With him each one of us felt "unbearable lightness of being." He held our attention with the most profound lectures on the spiritual destiny of man without making us feel like louts. At the same time, he enjoyed a good joke, appreciated women and beauty, and loved good food, coffee, and an occasional cigarette.

Friedemann had a brain tumor which his doctors in the US were not too optimistic about and he was here to find a faith healer. "You mean, a highly educated Western man like you believes in those things?" we asked. He explained that in reality it is not the faith healer who does the healing: it is us. A faith healer is simply someone who is very good at being a channel for divine energy to flow to the sick person so he can heal himself. (In fact, many faith healers are not very spiritual persons.) Can we really heal ourselves? The reality around us—ideas, sensory experience, even illness— is "given" by our habitual way of thinking, Friedemann said. We participate in the divine task of creation when we become imaginative and intuitive human beings—when we bring in something "not given." Art and transcendental experience, including what we think of as "miracles," are always from the "not given." (P.S.: Friedemann was cured, but his faith healer died within the year.)

It was surely from my "not given" that through a marvelous string of events I awoke one morning in a cradle of lushest green, the incredibly pure music of crickets and cicadas still ringing in my ears. We were a small group of middle-aged suburbanites who had been drawn to this yoga workshop in Sta. Lucia, a barrio at the foothills of mystic Mount Banahaw. Our teacher was Ciay M., a gorgeous and gifted Filipina based in Boston, who comes home once a year to share the good news of a painless, free-form yoga. For five days, Ciay led us in daily loosening up, just moving where our bodies wanted to go. Her yoga was not concerned with achieving poses but with untensing the body by breathing through the back belly, like a baby. Seeing her gracefully ascend mountain paths like a doe, we understood that the aches and pains of our slouchy bodies—stiff necks, aching backs, weak muscles, painful joints, and excess weight—kept us from loving ourselves and becoming happy, fulfilled, self-confident human beings.

One afternoon we climbed the hill called Kalbaryo in time to catch the sunset. Like folk pilgrims, we prayed at the foot of the three crosses where candles sputtered in the wind, and love messages had been laid to rest in the earth's crevices. Watching the sunset from a rock, glorious light above and splendor of green below, I fell naturally into a meditative mood. I closed my eyes and a picture came vividly to me:

> *I was a fish swimming in the Sta. Lucia River, but I was unhappy. I longed to be something more. People walked and ran along the forest trail by the riverbank—how beautiful they were with their powerful brown bodies and their strong legs! I splashed around and leapt up and down in the water trying to keep pace with them. "Wait for me," I cried. "Please take me with you. Don't leave me behind," I pleaded. But no one heard me. They disappeared into the trees around the bend, and I was alone in the water, my heart breaking with soundless sobs.*

Suddenly, my whole body was racked with pain. All over the valley my moan of anguish rent the air. Something vital was touched: something broke and turned loose. I wept and wept uncontrollably—for all that could not be, for songs unsung, for time gone by, for secrets untold, for stars unseen, for dreams lost and doors closed and loves forgotten. And slowly I began to let go.

The next day, in the upland waters of Kinabuhayan, which nourish the precious springs of Santissima, we laughed and played like children, balancing on mossy stones, delighting in the fragile beauty of leaves and wildflowers. With awe we realized that as we opened our minds and bodies to the ancient wisdom of yoga, we were filled with the grace of nature and the spirit of Banahaw. The physical leads to the metaphysical. Awareness of breath leads to awareness of body leads to awareness of self. It was an easy next step to take Ciay's wise and earnest advice: that we each spend some time meditating alone in one of the many caves that serve as places of worship to the faithful of the mountain. In the cathedral cave of *Ina ng Awa,* we let the loving darkness embrace us, and we yearned to float in the nothingness forever.

Through the homey Montelibano cottage came and went all manner of people engaged in mystical-psychic pursuits, drawn by the spiritual energy of Banahaw. There was Mang Ed, once at death's door, now cured of emphysema, who gave us our first lessons in pranic healing. There was Ruben, heir to the folk *oracion* tradition, who, with a warm whiff of breath on my crown chakra, sent me mind-traveling to the crater of Mount Banahaw (which takes a good climber two days), where I saw the three waterfalls exactly as the locals describe them—golden red, white, and blue. There was a woman speaking in someone else's voice who suddenly fell over in a trance, stiff as board. All of this benignly overseen by the two resident warlocks, truth-seekers, and self-confessed "path of indulgence" followers: Boy F., esoteric *arbularyo* and devotee to the Earthly Mother; and Boy M., rogue-turned-seer of human nature. With unflagging energy and aplomb, they kept the whole household up until the wee hours with raunchy tales and eclectic views on life, love, and the spirit. (Drop the ego, I kept reminding myself, drop the ego.)

There I also came to know Riza R., who wears caftans and turkish pants and does healing work with crystals. Crystals are made of the same stuff as we are—sand and water—Riza explained, but because of their molecular structure they vibrate at a very precise rate (and thus are used in watches, radios, computers, and lasers), amplifying, transforming, storing, and focusing energy. They help the healing process along by opening up our blocked channels of energy so that our cells can get oxygen to rebuild themselves. Our thoughts are a refined form of energy, so crystals can affect them as well. But the important thing to remember is that crystals are only aids, not substitutes, for the inner work we all have to do to heal ourselves and grow.

Of course, kings and emperors, who have always crowned themselves with jewels, and even popes and cardinals, who have us kiss their rings, have always known the power of gems and crystals. And since I have always loved gems, if not to own, at least to feel their sensuous shapes and wrap my tongue around their wondrous-sounding names—amethyst, rose quartz, sapphire, tiger's eye, tourmaline, citrine, garnet, lapis lazuli, carnelian, moonstone— I lay quiet while Riza covered me with crystals and we told each other the stories that women tell of their lives.

Riza invited me to join a crystal camp in Bukidnon that summer, and I enticed Tita, a fellow teacher and good-time chaser, to come along. It was a complete fiasco. The organizer came up with zero what he had advertised in his brochure. So as darkness fell, we ten tired sojourners resigned ourselves to our makeshift shelter in the heart of a forest, eating fish and rice off banana leaves, and huddling unwashed in our sleeping bags.

That night, to ward off our depression and shield us from danger, Riza led the group in white light meditation. Then to our amazement, Jinky started describing the dwarfs and fairies she could see all around, and scribbling line after line of frenzied writing on yellow pad paper. When Frank deciphered it for us, it was a long, touching message of welcome and protection from the earth elementals, expressed in the most lyrical archaic Tagalog. We had all been together many centuries ago, they said, in a fairy kingdom in this forest, and they were happy that we were all together once again. It was a beautiful story...so that's why we're here...I was a fairy princess...once upon a time...and we all fell into delicious sleep.

What a thrill we got the next morning when, following the sounds of rushing water, we came upon a crystal clear river, strewn with huge boulders over which waterfalls crashed and cascaded. Without a thought, we threw off our clothes and plunged into the icy waters. And in our pure, baby-like nakedness we knew once more what bliss was like.

If our university friends could see us now, Tita and I mused. Two middle-aged women, no husbands with five-star ideas to protect and caution us for a change, we were ferried on motorcycles over muddy roads and precarious ridges, the sight of living bluegreen mountains all around slamming the breath out of us. We trudged for hours over a rugged trail to a cave where we were supposed to mine our own quartz crystals, but the trail got narrower and steeper as we ascended, and reluctantly we turned back. The next morning we left for Malaybalay, empty-handed. To console ourselves, we spent a couple of days treasure-hunting in the exotic markets of Cagayan de Oro, where Tita paid a small fortune for two fabulous antique *malongs*.

C. was beginning to worry about all this belated footlooseness. "You are not the woman I married," he fretted. Friends scolded me for overdoing the "flowing" bit. Only my children seemed to enjoy hearing about my adventures and appreciating the more relaxed and good-natured me. But I never had any doubt that it was all leading me to a good place. I just knew when the time was right everything would converge, and I would emerge renewed. One by one I felt all the issues that had bugged me being addressed and falling away. It was the freest, most joyful time of my life.

With the help of a dream counselor, my dreams began to speak to me more and more. One I took to be about major midlife issues:

C. and I were in a public place teeming with people, somewhat like a provincial sports stadium or cockpit. (The atmosphere was masa.) I wanted to step out for a while and was making my way through the crowd when a young man blocked my path. He was a lanky youth, about twenty years old, with a hostile look and piercing eyes. I said, "Makikiraan nga," and he faced me squarely and said, "Hinahamon kita." Without batting an eyelash, I accepted the challenge. (My dream ego seemed androgynous—I felt both male and female in the dream.)

We stepped outside. The contest consisted of his clinging to the wooden enclosure of the stadium with his hands and feet, like a monkey, while I tried to pry him loose. As I pulled long and hard, he stretched and stretched like a rubber man, while still managing to hang on. But he knew he was losing, and he kept looking at me with hurt and angry eyes. Finally, he couldn't hold on any longer. I pulled him loose completely. We didn't say anything to each other. He just looked and looked at me sullenly and walked away. My attitude towards him was tolerant, like

that of a parent towards an impulsive child. I felt I had put him
in his place, that he had gotten what he asked for. I sensed no
anger towards him at all. I went back inside the stadium and
rejoined C., who smiled at me proudly for having taken care of
that bit of business.

Who is the young man I struggled with and defeated? In Jungian dreamwork, he could be the *puer aeternus,* the part of us that refuses to grow up. Not the wholesome, playful child in us we must always try to keep, but the undisciplined narcissist that cannot commit to anything, whether work or relationship. Like an adolescent rebelling against parental discipline, I was feeling restricted by my marriage and family responsibilities. (My favorite battlecry at this time was: "My God, I'm forty-five years old! Why do you treat me like a child? Why can't I do what I want?") Perhaps my dream was saying I had the inner capacities to free myself from the hold of immature impulses and achieve full-adult status. But I had to fight this battle alone, without the protective father/husband to help me. It was a powerful affirmation of my deepest intuitions.

A GREAT COMFORT as one goes through midlife is the companionship of women. I experienced this when my sister Bette came for a visit after many years abroad. Although we had not corresponded much over the years, we were undergoing the same process and discovering the same things. Her path was through Unity, a free-style Christian church in the US, which had led her and her family to rediscover their spiritual selves. She had initiated the drastic move to the US (it was probably the start of her own midlife crisis) feeling harassed, confused, and stuck. Now I was overjoyed to see her so happy and all together, looking as young as when we were college girls in Maryknoll thirty years before.

We could not bear to be parted for one minute. We took our showers together, stayed in the john together, lingered over breakfast, lunch, and dinner, unable to talk of anything else but this most exciting of quests—the quest for ourselves—and at last asking the essential questions. What was our mission in life? Why had we married these guys? Why had we chosen these parents? Why had our children chosen us?

We shared endless stories about our life-teachers and what we had learned from them. I loved what one of her teachers had said: we are not human beings trying to be spiritual; we are spiritual beings undergoing a human experience. When I expressed lingering dissatisfaction with some aspects of my life, she said, "We are the authors of our lives. Look at your home, your family, your friends—you have created beauty all around you." Her own life issues had all confronted her at midlife: her husband's now courageously overcome alcoholism; her frustration at being unable to live an artist's life; her stressful clashes with her supervisor; her childhood resentments against our parents; her swings between affection and anger towards her children: all, she realized, were paths to her spiritual growth, sources of strength and stability in the gracefully unfolding story of her life. I was tremendously inspired.

As I approached my forty-sixth birthday, I made a bold decision: to give up my academic tenure of fourteen years (significantly, two seven-year cycles). I had been going back and forth on the question for a year, for from the point of view of calculating intellect resigning didn't make much sense. By university standards, I was ripe for a promotion and for a stronger leadership role in my department. But that no longer held much attraction for me. What mattered was no longer the attainment of goals, but the process of living. And part of that process, I now deeply understood, was shedding things along the way, just as our bodies slough off old cells and make new ones.

C. and I celebrated our twenty-first wedding anniversary (the end of three seven-year cycles) with a once-in-a-lifetime European jaunt with our four girls, Nini, Joanna, Ivi and Resa. When C. had to leave us in Vienna to fly to the US on business, Nini and I took a big bus to newly reopening Budapest. There, on a bright spring weekend, we celebrated her twentieth birthday hunting for antique bottles and downing goulash and chicken paprika.

And for dessert I went off by myself to the US East Coast, where, for the first time in eighteen years, my father and all eight of us brothers and sisters were reunited in one place. Though we are all of different religious persuasions (Marc and Gina are R.C., Bette is Unity, Raquel was Buddhist then Mormon and is now Born Again, Dave is Mormon, Leila is Anglican, Pat seems agnostic, and I may be Taoist-Christian), we all agree on one thing: health.

So we lazed away our days in a borrowed beach house, lying on the sand, playing with the little ones, doing *qi-gong* to New Age music, swapping *Fit for Life* recipes, discussing the connection between long-held resentment and cancer (which runs in our family), munching on ripe peaches and sunflower seeds, and scooping up spinach and arugula, lettuce and watercress, endives and baby corn at the supermarket. For our final repast, my *hijada* Ana Lea, Bette's eldest, had us all dipping into a communal pot of sticky rice and rolling thousands of *sushi*, which, after all that, disappeared in a flash.

When had I last enjoyed that incomparable feeling of just being myself? I had almost forgotten that once upon a time I had belonged to a place of absolute comfort and acceptance called home. If mid-life is a time for healing life's wounds, this was wonderful medicine. For weeks after I got back to Manila, I had recurring dreams of wandering in and out of airports with my siblings, as if my astral body had tarried behind with them.

HAVING TAMED the rat-racer in me, I began to accept some writing projects that could lead me to My Career, Part II. Then in my own time I went back to teaching, not the same old things but an interdisciplinary course of my own design which I called "Holistic Studies." Twenty graduating college seniors were my willing conspirators in this adventure, which started with us getting comfortable with ourselves through breath awareness and free body movement; doing a walking meditation around the campus, kissing the earth with our feet; learning how to incubate and interpret our dreams; confronting and letting go of our hurts and pains; and feasting on soul food in a vegetarian restaurant.

But not before we had stumbled over our mental blocks to establish that this flaky-sounding stuff had solid backing in the hard sciences, which began to move towards a New Paradigm after Einstein led the way to quantum mechanics. According to his heirs, the New Physicists, the physical properties we observe in the external world are enmeshed in our own perceptions. (It's all in the mind, after all.) What we perceive as more or less solid matter is composed, not of analyzable elementary particles, but of sets of relationships that reach outward to other things. (We are empty if not in relationships.) Everything, including our thoughts, is made up of networks of energy. (Vibes are real !) Furthermore, we are not just detached observers; whenever we observe a phenomenon, we change it. What we experience is not "external" reality but the interaction of our "I" with it. (It's a participatory universe.)

Stanford neuroscientist Karl Pribram supports this with his brain research, which connects behavioral science with theoretical physics. The universe is a hologram, he states. Our individual brains are bits of the hologram so they have access to all the information in the total system. (IQ belongs to the Old Paradigm and has nothing to do with this.) Our mental processes are made of the same stuff as the basic organizing principle of the universe. (Are we thinking, or are we being thought?) Our thoughts or consciousness creates reality and affects events. (Prayers and curses work.) The more orderly or coherent your mind is (more loving, less fearful), the more attuned you are to the primary level of reality. Meaningful "coincidences," psychic, paranormal, and mystical experiences are therefore not unnatural, for they derive from the purposeful connectedness of everything, which transcends time and space. (We all have ESP.)

By no coincidence, this fits in perfectly with University of London physicist David Bohm's theory of implicate order which states that, although it may not be readily apparent, there is an order enfolded into the very process of the universe. (Even the Calauan murders are in Divine Order???) It is only our divisive thinking that makes us see dividedness in reality, and experience it in fragments. Actually, the nature of reality is unbroken wholeness, and everything is intimately connected at a deep and fundamental level. (In postmodern aesthetics, incongruity is in the eye of the beholder.) Hence the cure for the ills of the world must begin with healthier (wholistic) thinking.

Among all these, my favorite is 1977 Nobel Prize winner for chemistry Ilya Prigogine's theory of dissipative structures, which provides a scientific model for transformation. Everything in nature, even a rock or a crystal, is a dance of electrons, Prigogine says, constantly vibrating in response to and in harmony with the environment. (We are always in process.) The more complex a structure, the more subject to stress and the greater its potential for attaining a higher order of existence. (If you're more stressed than me, you must be smarter?) In human beings, this forward shift may be provoked by inward attention (meditation, reverie, relaxation), which increases the slower brainwaves known as alpha and theta and generates a larger fluctuation in the brain. And what's more, each new level is more integrated than the one before. (Growth is habit-forming.)

Actually, we don't need scientists to tell us what we have already discovered for ourselves: that pain and stress often force us to change; that to change our reality we have to change our innermost thoughts; that before we can create something, we must experience chaos; that the most beautiful people we know are those who have gone through suffering and conflict.

According to New Age thinkers and researchers, all of this sounds very much like old Eastern mysticism. "Is it a coincidence," asks Gary Zukav in *The Dancing Wu Li Masters* (1979), "that Buddhists exploring 'internal' reality a millennium ago and physicists exploring 'external' reality a millennium later both discovered that 'understanding' involves passing the barrier of paradox?" The physics curricula of the twenty-first century, he predicts, will include classes in meditation.

I KNOW I have a long way to go, but in this epic journey of my midlife, being on the way is the point. Moment by moment I feel I am in flux and I am glad I no longer feel bound by traditional options. As part of higher-order life, I am capable of "boundless innovation and alternate realities."

When I was younger, I used to say that I was not afraid of dying, only of growing old. Today, I feel I have conquered many of my fears, including aging. I have touched a snake, experienced acupuncture, and gone without makeup. I now find it corny to be coy about one's age. I want to be more of a truth-teller. Like the wise old crone of myth, I get the urge to do the "kind/cruel" thing, such as when I see a colleague vainly combing his hair over a bald spot and I want to go up to him, gently brush back the silly-looking strand, and say, "It's okay, my dear, it's okay to just be yourself."

Things I used to take for granted now fill me with a sense of gratitude and wonder. When things "go my way" and I am able to keep all my appointments and do all my errands without a hitch, I know I must be in tune with everything else—and my mind boggles at the tremendous confluence of forces required to make that happen. Grace, says a New Age writer, is co-operating with the life source itself.

Knowing myself and the nature of the universe a little better makes me more aware of my powers and potentials (but also of my vulnerabilities). I no longer hold them back when I think they can help. Anxious-looking faces inside an ambulance careening through the thickets of traffic move me and I murmur, "The Force be with you!" Gifts of food which constantly fill our table lift me up in blessing. Bette falls ill in the US and I send her my healing energy.

It seems to me criminal to do things in a hurry, unenlightened to feel harassed. C. and friends all around are turning fifty; I have become a crusader for the art of slowing down. Driving by a vacant city lot, I halt, totally transfixed by the sight of a playful wind whirling dry leaves and grasses in a dusty jig. C. and the girls and I are stretched out on a darkened beach in Bohol, and our Easter is made holy when we see a huge star fall brightly across the sky for a magical instant.

Chatting in the breakfast nook, my four girls tell me about this pop group with the brilliant name of Soul Asylum whose first hit song is called "Runaway Train." The video flashes faces of missing children on the screen, with the result that several have been reunited with their families. We passionately agree it is our life's ambition to be able to thus combine art, fun, success, and service. I have no doubt that a new belief system among our children will bring about a new type of political force and the kind of leaders we want.

Not just a century but an age is coming to a close. Around the year 2035 the sun is calculated to complete another leg in its 25,000-year journey through the twelve constellations of the zodiac. The cataclysmic changes that we are now witnessing, sages say, are signs of the dawning of a New Age of peace, harmony, and love. I am thrilled to be part of orderly and meaningful creation, in which one of the primary laws is cyclical and progressive change. The whole universe is midlifing— and I, a droplet in a ripple in the multigalactic energy sea, am swimming mindfully along with it.

THE SPIRITUAL JOURNEY

JUDETTE A. GALLARES, r.c.

When I have ceased to break my wings
Against the faultiness of things,
And learned that compromises wait
Behind each hardly opened gate,
When I can look Life in the eyes,
Grown calm and very coldly wise,
Life will have given me the Truth,
And taken in exchange — my youth.
"Wisdom" by Sara Teasdale

I WAS forty-two and very much a midlifer when I chanced upon this poem. Sara Teasdale expressed for me at that time the challenge and invitation I felt to reassess my life in the light of who I was and who I was meant to be. I was then in

93

the midst of putting my life together again after practically "breaking my wings" as a worker in God's vineyard and in the process depleting myself of psychic and spiritual energies. Thank God there is such a reality as "midlife transition," a harbinger of Truth which invites us to "look Life in the eyes" and to be at peace with it.

What is midlife transition? What are its manifestations, themes, and spiritual challenges? How should prayer and spirituality be approached at this time of one's life? These are some of the questions I wish to explore as I reflect on how my personal experience of midlife has invited me to come into a greater knowledge and acceptance of myself and a deeper relationship with God.

My experience of midlife transition actually began ten years earlier, when I found myself facing some sort of a "crisis of limits." I was thirty-two, had made final vows in the Cenacle congregation, and had had experience in the apostolate for nine years. I had gained confidence in my abilities as a retreat and spiritual director and could facilitate a program for just about any group that showed up at the retreat house. But I was bored. The question formed in my mind, "What am I doing in this congregation if I no longer like its work, when I am no longer challenged by it, when I often feel 'sick and tired' of it?" My call to religious life was not in question, but I was bewildered. I didn't feel like directing anyone's retreat or spiritual life; I didn't want to listen to anyone's woes; I felt at times that I was even more needy than those who came to me with their problems; I wasn't interested in being with people, much less conducting group programs; I didn't even feel like singing or playing the guitar for liturgies. I didn't feel attracted to ministry — at all!

This "crisis" had psychological manifestations (little things irritated me and I tended to be emotionally sensitive). It also had physical repercussions (I was always tired and easily caught colds). But I sensed that its roots were spiritual, for the ultimate question it asked was "What is the meaning of my life?" At that time, I did not know why I continued to pray. My immediate experience of prayer was dryness, emptiness, and desolation, but somehow my whole life at that moment was my prayer. Beyond this there was an obscure sense that the Lord *was*. My intuition was that the answer to my dilemma lay in the spiritual realm, just like the earlier transitions I had experienced, especially the transition from adolescence to young adulthood, when I discovered that my relationship with God was at the very heart of my quest for meaning.

Recalling my earlier transitions helped put things in perspective for me. I remembered my young adulthood experience when I encountered a more personal God in my life. It was, paradoxically, at a time when I was farthest from the church. The prayers I learned as a child were no longer appropriate expressions of where I was as a young adult and of the relationship I then wanted desperately to have with a noninstitutional God. I realized that God who was seemingly absent, was present all along. Having hurdled that transition and discovered Christ present in my life, I knew at thirty-two that I could live with seeming meaninglessness on the surface of my life if I could come back over and over to God and say, "To whom shall I go? You alone have the words of eternal life" (Jn 6:68).

But life transitions are not completed overnight. Nor are they a "once and for all" kind of task. At forty-two, I thought I would no longer be beset by similar questions I had encountered when I was thirty-two about the meaning of my life. Although conditions and circumstances were totally different, what was at the heart of my questions was my spiritual quest, my relationship with the divine.

REFLECTING on these experiences helped me understand not only myself but also others in their transition years who have since come to me for guidance and direction. I believe that midlife is a time and an opportunity God offers every person to reappraise, review and reevaluate his or her life so he or she can come to a greater degree of integration and fulfillment and so that more realistic expectations may be arrived at for the future.

In my experience guiding and directing the prayer life of other adults, I have noticed that many of them (in their late thirties and in their forties and fifties) are again raising issues resolved years earlier

— and supposedly settled forever — and are searching for some direction in their life journey. Confronted with personal finiteness and the inevitability of approaching death, especially in their experience of losing someone close to them or the realization of the diminishment of their capacities, many people are forced to reconsider how they understand themselves and their lives, what will make them happy, and what will give their lives continued meaning. Some handle midlife calmly and smoothly; others experience considerable upheaval which may be considered a "midlife crisis." Still others may not even be aware of it or may not allow any self-questioning or reflection to enter the realm of their consciousness. But for everyone there is definitely a "midlife transition," a change or process which characterizes this cycle in life. No one is exempt from it for it is part of the human cycle and quest for meaning.

But each of our spiritual passages is unique. No two people experience their midlife transition in exactly the same way. Aside from our unique personalities, which make our experiences of transition distinct from one another, culture, gender, and socioeconomic level add further nuances to the way we experience this cycle. Midlife transition is not an "elitist" phenomenon. It may not be part of the vocabulary and consciousness of the poor, whose daily preoccupation is survival, but in the midst of their struggle they often articulate the question, *Ganito na lang ba ang buhay? Kayod nang kayod?* It is a spiritual question for it ultimately asks, "What is the meaning of my life? What is the meaning of existence?" One does not have to be rich to ask deeply spiritual questions.

MIDLIFE transition is not only a contemporary phenomenon. Literature from many different historical periods, even if it does not specifically use the term *midlife*, describes this human experience of change with emptiness and meaninglessness or with confusion and disorientation. For instance, in his "Inferno," Dante Alighieri describes this period of life in the following manner:

> *In the middle of the journey of our life*
> *I came to myself within a dark wood*

Where the straight way was lost.

Darkness and the journey are images frequently used by people to describe their experience of a religious mid life transition, like John of the Cross' "dark night," which has become a common phrase to describe a period in one's life when one questions the goals and the meaning of life.

Yet this feeling of being lost in the journey or being in darkness, which causes different degrees of anxiety in midlifers, is not the whole story of the middle years. It simply marks the beginning of a transition, of a passage on an unfamiliar road, of an encounter with one's true self. In her book *Gift from the Sea,* Anne Morrow Lindbergh speaks of her experience of the middle years as a time of shedding shells — the shell of ambition, the shell of material accumulations and possessions, the shell of the ego. This shedding, which feels like darkness and loss, is a fearsome journey, but it can be the liberation by which we become, at last, completely ourselves. Probing her inner experience, she writes, "One is afraid. Naturally. Who is not afraid of pure space — that breathtaking empty space of an open door? But despite fear, one goes through to the room beyond." Reflecting further on what mid life is all about, Lindbergh asks, "Could midlife not be a time when we are free at last for enhancing mind, heart, and talent; free at last for spiritual growth?"

A whole body of literature probing the different aspects of midlife transitions arrives at the same question Lindbergh asked and affirms that the midlife journey is truly a spiritual journey towards the integration, renewal, and transformation of the inner self. As such, the freedom for spiritual growth is perceived as God's renewed call to conversion by reconciling ourselves with our past and by allowing our self-understanding to be challenged and relativized so that we may find our deeper self in God. As one author articulates it, "The mid life transition is an experience of personal and social fragmentation that opens the way for a new level of spiritual interpretation." But this is a scary process. Anything involving change is always met with resistance. We are constantly afraid of what we will uncover and discover and what it will demand from us. We are afraid to be still and

97

to be quiet. Instead we fill our life with possessions and our time with constant activity and chatter in an attempt to silence our inner longings and gnawings. Slowly do we realize that time for solitude and silence is needed for the process of change and transformation to begin taking root in our life. T.S. Eliot succinctly expresses this spiritual challenge in his poem "East Coker":

I said to my soul, be still,
And let the dark come upon you
Which shall be the darkness of God.

From the way writers and poets describe this experience of darkness in the journey, midlife is not merely a phase in one's life but rather an invitation to faith and a time of faith. In the darkness we learn to believe, no matter how fragile our faith may be, that God is present in spite of the seeming divine absence. It is a solitary faith where we meet God in our aloneness, a unifying faith where we gather our self together in making an act of faith as we entrust ourselves to an unseen and unexperienced God.

Even psychologists and psychotherapists recognize that spiritual and faith issues are more prominent at midlife. Carl Jung, a recognized pioneer in the study of midlife, found that religious questioning was often a central dilemma in the midlife search of people he had treated. He remarked that among all his patients in the second half of life, there had not been one whose problem in the last resort was not that of finding a religious outlook on life. Developmental psychologists have followed Jung's lead. They also describe midlife transitions as religious passages because spirituality at this point seeks to bring the wealth of our faith tradition upon this human experience. For instance, at this junction in life we are more ready to believe that in the light of Christ's Incarnation God is found within, not apart from, human life, and that God's vision for each person is to be whole and integrated.

At midlife we are thus invited and challenged to take the next step in our faith development, which is a step towards wholeness or holiness. Taking this step is essential to our spiritual journey. This religious quest in the second half of life is not necessarily dramatic.

It may only be a quiet, interior pursuit. On the one hand, those who never showed interest in religion before or have relegated it to the background in their drive for worldly success may begin showing signs of interest in it. On the other hand, religious people may become frustrated at midlife by the apparent emptiness of theological concepts even if, for many years, they have felt satisfied with the vision of life which these concepts conveyed. But the root of this frustration or restlessness is a search for a more dynamic understanding of theology, of Christian life, and of themselves. They desire a deeper relationship with God and a more authentic living out of their religious vocation.

This was the way I, as a religious, began to experience midlife. The life of commitment to God I had lived for ten years when I was thirty-two suddenly became tasteless. I longed for a much simpler and more authentic witnessing of my religious commitment which would not be dependent on how much knowledge or experience I had amassed, on how successful I was in the ministry, or on how many people I had brought closer to God. These are self-centered desires and ambitions which tend to mask themselves as good and which stem from unmet or unconscious needs. Realizing that I had so many of these, I felt the need for God's healing grace, a healing that would touch the very roots of my being, so that I would no longer rely on my own accomplishments but only on God's grace. Paradoxically, it was in my acknowledgement of my own sinfulness and need for God's healing forgiveness that I began to feel whole again and one with Christ in his own experience of the Father's compassion, love, and mercy. But my midlife process was far from over and this palpable experience of God's grace did not last long. Feelings of dissatisfaction with myself, the tastelessness of religious traditions and practices would return. I realized that God's call to wholeness and holiness is to be heeded continually each day. But in my human frailty, I, like the rest of humanity, tend to turn a deaf ear to God's call. I sometimes ask myself why this is so and why God's call is always met with resistance and inner struggle. This pattern of resistance seems to be present even in the lives of biblical characters and saints.

My studies and reflection have slowly enlightened me on the meaning and implications of God's call to holiness. This call is part of our ongoing conversion where we are constantly drawn towards greater openness to the truth, to the good, and ultimately, to God. This involves giving up longheld ideas and practices, and parting with and accepting the past. But what makes conversion difficult is the pain connected with it, the pain of "dying to self," which often reaches overpowering proportions at midlife. Yet "death to self" brings with it an end to the bondage which we create for ourselves in accordance with our own self-made image and self-definition. Based on how we have tried to live our life according to society's or our family's expectations, the call to "die to self" means differently to people. To women, this "death to self" may mean learning to appreciate themselves more and gaining more confidence in their gifts as persons. It also implies taking stock of who they are and what will bring them a greater or fuller life after living a life of sacrifice and self-donation for the sake of their children or families. To men, however, "death to self" may mean more of an uprooting of self-centered desires, projects, and ideas that have driven them away from their true selves and their significant relationships. It also implies an acceptance that one cannot always take dominion over the whole world and that a grasping, controlling stance in life does not always bring the meaning and happiness one seeks. Considering that women develop mainly by way of attachment and that they form their identity in relationships with others, at midlife a woman may be challenged to integrate a stronger concern for herself into her service and compassion for others. Men, on the other hand, may be led from self-reliance, autonomy, and domination to greater attachment and concern for others.

From whatever perspective we may understand the call to "die to self," one thing is clear: it implies a movement against the ego and towards a fuller life and a strengthening of what we may consider weak in us. It calls us to grow in acceptance of ourselves, including the less attractive features and dark aspects of our personality and personal history which we would prefer to keep out of our awareness.

100

Paradoxically, it is often through confrontation with our darker side that we find occasion to overcome the divisions which exist inside of us and begin to experience greater integration of self. This confrontation with the truth of who we are, which in effect leads us to a fuller acceptance of our whole self, is one step along the way to a closer relationship with God. The closer we are to truth, the closer we are to God, for God is Truth.

The call to wholeness or holiness in the journey of conversion is also a call to experience the fullness of life. This is what Jesus offers when he says in John's Gospel, "I have come to give you life, life in its fullness" (Jn 10:10). But first we have to empty ourselves in order to be filled by God. At midlife, as described above, there can be a growing realization that what used to satisfy us in the past, which comes to us through our work, activities, relationships, and possessions, often leaves us empty. We are thus invited to let go and empty ourselves of this false sense of fullness and security so we may be filled with the fullness of God.

SUCH Is God's invitation in the Book of Ruth, which tells us the story of two women who went through life transitions. Let us examine the story more closely and glean from it a few insights about the spiritual journey God is continually inviting us to embark on.

In the Book of Ruth, we see a powerful demonstration of the movement from emptiness to fullness as a paradigm of conversion during life transitions. The theme of emptiness and fullness is seen not only in the setting of the story itself but also in the lives of the main female characters, Ruth and Naomi. The famine or the emptiness of the land that sets the story in motion drives Naomi's family to seek "greener pastures." Leaving one's country and culture is an experience of emptying akin to an experience of loss —not only loss of food in time of famine, but also loss of relationships and of property and land. To a certain extent, it recalls a recurring motif in the life of Israel and all throughout salvation history which began with God inviting Abraham to leave his clan and his ancestral home for a promised land. In Abraham we saw that God's promise and blessing are indissolubly bound up with a departure, an emptying of anything that prevents one from setting out on an adventure with God. But to Naomi, Moab turned out to be not a land of promise but a place of emptiness. There she lost not only her husband but later her two sons as well. Her emptiness seemed irreparable, her life so hollow deep within. Like the psalmist, these words could have echoed in Naomi's heart: "How could we sing a song to the Lord in a foreign land?" (Ps. 137:4, New American Bible)

It would be difficult indeed for anyone in Naomi's predicament to sing a song to God when one feels alienated from God, life, others, and even self. Based on our human experience, our capacity to pray is greatly influenced by what we experience in our body and spirit. We also know that grief has a way of devouring our spiritual life, leaving us in the desert to feel parched, empty, depleted, lonely, and alienated.

Naomi could only attribute the cause of her incurable emptiness to God ("Yahweh's hand has been raised against me!"). Thus, only God also could fill it. Beyond her empty feeling and sense of God's absence is perhaps a fragile hope that God will also cause her misery to cease. Perhaps this was in her mind and heart when the narrator says: "Having heard that Yahweh had come to help his people by giving them food, Naomi prepared to return home."

In her poverty her emptiness was so basic — expressed only in her hunger for food. But perhaps beyond this need to fill her physical hunger was a keen desire to reconcile herself with the past, to catch a glimpse of home and the possibility of who she was meant to be. John Dunne wrote:

> At every turn in the road
> a new illuminating is needed to find the way
> and a new kindling is needed to follow the way.

Dunne seems to speak here of moments of transition in one's life when one needs to search within to find illumination or guidance so as to continue going forward on the road to life. This search within one's self essentially involves the movement to return to the past — to one's home and roots — and to be reconciled with it.

Naomi, in her poverty and emptiness, thought of home not only as a place where she could experience God's blessing again ("having heard that Yahweh had come to help his people") but also as a place where she could find peace and acceptance of her painful situation ("Don't call me Naomi. Call me Mara for Yahweh has made life bitter for me.") This movement is reflective of a deep longing that is present in every human heart. A part in us is always yearning, longing, and quietly crying out for the true homeland where life is no longer painful and unfair.

Undoubtedly, Naomi's two Moabite daughters-in-law were also experiencing emptiness and grief at losing their husbands. In their loss, their initial response was to cling to what was familiar (to continue living with Naomi and to remain in her clan) even if it did not seem to give them any kind of future. Orpah was practical minded in dealing with her emptiness. In spite of the pain of saying good-bye to her relationships (with Naomi and Ruth) and to what had already become familiar to her, she heeded Naomi's advice and returned to her "mother's house." Perhaps she realized that life could still offer her a future in her own homeland. Or perhaps she also caught a glimpse of home and the possibility of who she could still become.

On the other hand, Ruth clung to her mother-in-law and took the risk of embracing her, her land, and her God even if the future was uncertain and seemingly bleak. Although Ruth too was going through transition, she offered Naomi her presence and companionship. Ruth felt for her mother-in-law because she too knew the pain of loss and the difficulty of adjusting to a new reality. But unlike Naomi, she was not going to allow this life transition to discourage or embitter her. For Ruth, the movement back to her mother's house seemed to be a movement away from what and who she was meant to be. Instead she followed the movement of Israel's first patriarch by leaving her homeland and venturing into the unknown. Like Abraham, she departed her homeland and emptied herself of anything that prevented her from setting out on an adventure with Abraham and Naomi's God. But unlike with Abraham, the God of Israel did not appear to Ruth with a promise and a blessing. She had none of these assurances. She left relying only on Naomi's God and the strength of her love for her mother-in-law. She dealt with her emptiness by further emptying herself so she could embrace totally the God of Abraham, of Naomi, and of Israel. She let go of the past in order to embrace the future with great faithfulness. And in these beautiful words which have become an immortal prayer of fidelity, she accompanied Naomi through her life transition:

> *Wherever you go, I will go, wherever you live, I will live. Your people shall be my people, and your God, my God. Wherever you die, I will die and there I will be buried. May Yahweh do this thing to me and more also, if even death should come between us!*
> (1:16-17, Jerusalem Bible)

Biblical fidelity, as we have seen in the Book of Ruth, recalls the faith of Israel that began with the departure of Abraham and ended with a covenant with God. It remembers the unique friendship established between God and Israel that is exemplified especially by Ruth. At the heart of this covenant fidelity was their faith that Yahweh was the God of life and therefore would call them to greater life.

Translated into the language and setting of today, faith calls us to face the light and to choose life, to empty ourselves of what is false in order to be filled with the truth. It enables us to look upon each "letting go" with trust and optimism and prepares us to face other, more painful relinquishments which commit us more fully to God's service. It enables us to catch a glimpse of who we are meant to be. Like Ruth and Naomi, faith urges us to move forward and embrace the God of life.

THE JOURNEY from emptiness to fullness as a paradigm of faith is essentially present in the Christian paradigm. St. Paul affirms this in his letter to the Philippians using an ancient christological hymn which tells of the pattern of salvation followed by Christ: though he was in the form of God, he emptied himself of his divinity to be like each one of us; in his human state, Christ obediently accepted death on the cross to save humankind from its bondage to sin; in this act of total emptying, God in turn highly exalted Christ and bestowed on him the name above every other name (cf. Phil.2:6-9). Jesus' dying and rising thus gives hope and meaning to every Christian life. To Jesus' followers, the way to victory is the way of the cross; the way to life is the acceptance of death. The letting-go of what is precious to us takes place not only at the end of our life but also in the many small deaths which are part of human growth. We let go and leave behind anything that does not free us to embrace the new. St. Paul expresses this sentiment in his first letter to the Corinthians. He says: "When I was a child, I spoke like a child, I thought like a child, I reasoned like a child. When I grew up, I gave up childish ways" (1 Cor.13:11). This is precisely the task and the invitation of every life transition — to leave behind "childish ways," including our childish images and ideas of God, in order to mature and deepen in our faith relationship with the divine. The way to this deeper faith is again the way of the cross which at midlife includes the challenge and invitation to face courageously the reality of our own death and finitude. From a Christian perspective, death then is seen as something positive, as a necessary element to accepting new life, our life in God. The cross that we must accept and carry is the Christian symbol of life coming through death and of light coming through darkness.

WE HAVE SEEN that aside from the midlife transition being a normal process and cycle of life which everyone must go through, midlife is primarily a spiritual journey, a journey towards integration and holiness. The divine invitation to embark on this journey is initially experienced through something which seems negative — a feeling of dissatisfaction, disorientation, tastelessness, restlessness, or questioning about the meaning of one's life. Yet it seems that it is only by passing through such an experience of personal and social fragmentation that the way to a new level of spiritual interpretation is opened up. We saw this process in biblical literature, especially in the Book of Ruth where the motif of emptiness and fullness symbolized the life transitions that the main characters, Ruth and Naomi, went through in their spiritual journey. We also saw that what helped them through their transitions was their commitment to companion each other. Biblical literature thus recognizes the importance of and need for spiritual companionship which is patterned after God's companionship with Israel when she went through her search for meaning and identity as a nation and people. Following the lead of Ruth and Naomi, we must not neglect the importance of seeking someone — a friend, a spiritual guide, or a counselor — to accompany us as we mourn our losses and limits, as we face our dark side to balance our polarities, and as we "die to our self" and discover a new way of living life more abundantly. Finally, this motif of emptiness and fullness, of loss and recovery, of death and new life, accentuated in the Book of Ruth is but a foreshadowing of the paschal mystery, of Christ's own death and resurrection, which is the Christian paradigm of faith. At midlife, God therefore invites us again to enter more deeply and fully into the meaning of the paschal mystery in our life and to experience in a more vibrant way the fullness of our personhood in Christ.

SUGGESTIONS FOR MIDLIFE SPIRITUALITY AND PRAYER

1. *Acknowledging our losses and limits.* At midlife, we no longer have a sense of unlimited time in which to reach or fulfill our goals and dreams. We start counting the years ahead rather than those behind. Even relationships have changed. They are no longer the friendships and marriages we had expected them to be. The tone of our prayer may be one of mourning, of "saying good-bye," of "letting go." Rather than deny the feelings that go with loss — such as sadness, anger, fear, guilt, and resentment — we acknowledge them. We can recall how Jesus mourned over Jerusalem as he realized that all his efforts to bring it to God seemed to have failed. Lamenting, he cried: O Jerusalem, Jerusalem, you slay the prophets and stone

106

those who are sent to you! How often have I wanted to gather your children together as a mother bird collects her young under her wings, and you refused me! (Lk 13:34)

In the spiritual life, the expression of our feelings of mourning is the path to emotional and spiritual wholeness. Experience tells us that the best way to deal with grief is to let it out, for mourning has its own rhythm of healing. Having a spiritual companion, a "soul friend," would help us mourn well. Keeping a journal may also help. Writing down our feelings of grief is a good way of acknowledging the difficult process we are going through. Ritualizing our losses or using symbolic action that expresses our feelings may also serve as a powerful support for mourning midlife losses. This can be done within the context of prayer or during a time of solitude or retreat. The book *Praying Our Good-byes* by Joyce Rupp, osm, contains helpful suggestions on the different ways of approaching grief.

2) *Embark on a spiritual journey.* According to Jung, midlife is a "turning within." To him, the full development of the authentic self is the task of the second half of life. Giving fuller attention to our spiritual life is part of this task. Interiorization therefore is the key movement of midlife spirituality. We cannot hold on to our childish ways of praying or to prayer forms that fed our spiritual life when we were younger. Developing or cultivating a life of contemplation becomes a challenge. This entails learning to be quiet, to listen to what stirs within us, to open ourselves up to God's presence in our life even if we might initially sense only an absence. This also involves our learning to wait attentively and patiently as we are gradually led to the truth of who we are. Having someone to share this process would be helpful. As suggested above, looking for a spiritual guide will help us learn ways of solitude and prayer. Making a one-on-one retreat might be helpful. Attending a seminar-retreat on midlife spirituality would also be beneficial.

3) *Recall earlier transitions and reflect on values and life patterns.* What have these transitions taught us? What were the questions then that we are again encountering now? Reflecting on these will help us to make a review and reassessment of our life in the context of God's

invitation to fuller life. The middle years are a time when we scrutinize our youthful vocational commitments and personal choices so that we can simplify them and bring them more in line with Christian values. What life directions for the second half of our life are surfacing for us?

4) *Integrate our inner divisions.* To integrate ourselves, we need to rebalance polarities. We discover that life does not have to be always an "either-or" but also an "and". There can be surprises behind compromises. Since the pull at midlife is towards wholeness, we experience a call to balance life's polarities: work and play, body and spirit, aloneness and togetherness, darkness and light, for example. By recognizing and accepting the darker side of our personality, i.e. our "shadow," we can learn to be more patient, compassionate, and loving not only to ourselves but also to others. This is prayer made concrete, spirituality brought into action.

THREE LETTERS

MARGARITA GO SINGCO-HOLMES, PH.D.

DEAR Dr. Holmes,

I wanted to commit suicide last night. That wasn't the first time the thought crossed my mind. It was just that last night's was so real, so intense, that now I am really frightened.

I am not some reckless teenager for whom talk of suicide is commonplace. I am a decent, responsible, and respectable woman of fifty-two who is both God-fearing and God-loving. That is why these suicidal thoughts are so frightening.

I wasn't always this way. I used to love my life, considering myself to be the luckiest woman in the world. It's not that I had everything. I didn't have a house in Forbes Park or a fancy car, but what I needed — and even some of the things I wanted — I had. All that seems to have changed and I can't even tell you why.

I don't know when I first started feeling this way. That in itself is rather strange since I am a great chronicler of emotional events. I can tell you when my husband and each of my five children started feeling one way or the other about things.

While I cannot tell you exactly *when* I started feeling this way, I know when I first started to notice it. It was the first of December, 1983. The kids were 9, 10, 11, 12, and 13. By that time they had all stopped believing in Santa Claus. Preparing for Christmas just wasn't the same. The kids themselves seemed less excited about it. I guess the certainty that one will get what one asked for from regular, flesh-and-blood parents is a bit of a letdown after writing to someone from the North Pole who rides on a big sleigh pulled by twelve reindeer.

I wonder now why I was so quick to relinquish the excitement that I felt then. At least then the kids were still excited about what I could give them, even if they weren't exactly mystified about *how* they got what they did. I remember that when they still believed in Santa Claus, they never stopped asking me how he could get into our house if we had no chimney for him to slide down. I finally told them Santa took his own chimney, precisely for houses like ours that had none—he wanted to make sure the security guards wouldn't mistake him for a thief, which they might have if he went in through an open window.

Now nothing I do seems to excite them anymore. They no longer hang on to my every word, no longer need me to wash their clothes or cook their food. They no longer ask me for advice or even for my opinions.

Sometimes they pretend they miss my cooking. They claim my *menudo* is the best they've ever tasted anywhere and that my *pancit* is incomparable. But even if they mean it, food is just not that important to them.

I don't know when I first started feeling like an invisible person. Invisible, as though I were never there. They never seem to look for me anymore. Instead I feel this palpable relief that they no longer have to "prop me up" during the rare times when they come home and I am talking to a friend or doing some gardening.

I guess that's what really hurts the most, that they have seen through me, through my desperate need of them, and know I am no longer the invincible mother I used to be to them. The fact that they

110

seem visibly relieved when I'm not moping hurts me too. I would never feel that way towards them, you see. I would be by their side in a minute if I felt they needed me. There would be no two ways about it. I would drop everything I had.

Not that they wouldn't. I have raised good kids. I have a good husband. But none of them would do it as automatically as I have, as I would. There would be some weighing of factors, even some wishful thinking: "Couldn't she have gotten sick on Saturday, after my big presentation?" or "I wonder if Dad could watch over Mom on Thursday so I could watch this concert with my friends." I am not complaining about this, merely hurt by it, and I don't know what to do about it!

I think what I feel most upset about is the fact that I live for my family and have never questioned the basic rightness of this decision. At least, not until last night. Does that mean my life has been empty? Does that make my life useless?

I had a job. I still have it, in fact, but it does not fill me with wonder and joy. It is not even useful, the way it used to be in the past. We used to need this second income from my job; we no longer do. I would quit this job, as my husband has asked me to do many times, but what would fill my time? In the past, there were the children I could've spent time with, but when they needed me most, I couldn't do it. How cruel life can be that now that I *do* have the luxury of time if I want it, I have no one and nothing to spend it on. What will I do, Dr. Holmes? Where will I go? What can I do to while away the time till my grandchildren come? I never realized waiting could be so painful!

This is not a sex problem, but I am hoping you will find the time to answer it soon. I am holding on as much as I can, but I know I cannot last much longer. Thank you and God bless you.

WAITING

Dear WAITING:

Thank you very much for your letter. It is interesting that you should choose WAITING as your pen name because that, of course, is exactly what you are doing. Not just in the *literal* sense of waiting for your grandchildren to be born, but also in the all-pervasive sense of waiting for your life to have meaning once again. And while it is a very *apt* description for you right now, it is also a rather sad one.

Not that there is anything wrong in waiting, in and of itself. There are some things worth waiting for. These are the same things worth living and fighting for. Somehow, I do not think grandchildren fall into this category. Again, it is not because I hate the sniveling little buggers. Quite the contrary. I am rather fond of baby smells, baby sounds, and even baby poo.

But to make other people's children the fulcrum of your whole life is just not a good idea. Among other things, it is something way beyond your control. What are you going to do? Tell your children to have children in the same way you told them many years ago to eat their vegetables and wipe their bottoms clean?

Besides, basing your whole life on other people's lives, no matter how cute, lovable and needy they are at the start, is an exercise in futility. The little ones eventually grow up and start having lives of their own, which might include you but will certainly not have you as the focus. At least not if you've done your job right .

As you have so painfully found out just recently.

You are the sort of person that needs to be needed. For the first half of your life, that was great because it dovetailed perfectly with what your husband's and children's needs were at the same time. But you have done your job well, so well that your children don't need you that much anymore, as well it should be, at least not in the same old way.

They do not need you in the same physical way they did before, but they do need you emotionally, even in ways they may not realize. For one thing, your daughters need you as a model of what a woman over fifty can be and can do. They need you to help them realize that women your age are a long way from "outliving their usefulness" and even farther away from losing their attractiveness as human beings. Your daughters need to learn from you in a way they never could from any newspaper column or TV show — that women over fifty have much to live for: friends, family, travel, poetry, painting, gardening, religion, spirituality, etcetera. Your sons need you too to serve as a beacon towards the kind of women they could have as wives—women who are attractive, joyful, and independent not only in their twenties but in their fifties, seventies and nineties as well.

But this, of course, is the wrong tack to take with you. Not that it won't work, of course. In fact, I can practically see you already sprucing yourself up and making plans so that indeed your children can see for themselves that in their fifties women need not be relegated to the wayside. I can see you joining women's clubs and throwing yourself into your job more so that you can angle for work that is more suited to your taste and/or your abilities.

But I am afraid that would be mistaking the forest for the trees. And while it would serve as a palliative — it would certainly stave off the depression you feel right now — it wouldn't really be solving the problem. It would just be more of the same thing: doing things for other people instead of for yourself.

Make no mistake. I am not taking back what I told you. Your children *do* need you still. Not as desperately as they did before in that they now can feed and clothe themselves. And certainly not as critically on the emotional level in that they can find other models of "happily mature women" should you be unable to provide a viable one for them. But need you they do. What they need from you is for you to be happy within yourself so that they don't have to think about you every single moment of their lives. It doesn't mean that they will disappear from your life entirely. Far from it. What it means is that when they *are* there, it's because they really want to be, and not because they are worried about you and you have guilt-tripped them into being there.

So where do you go from here? Back to square one, which is that you are the sort of woman that needs to be needed. You have done a marvelous job with your children and your husband. Your life was certainly not useless then and it certainly need not be useless now. All it needs is a change of focus. You can still opt to do the same thing,

113

respond to someone who needs you, but it seems to me that you can take a breather from the same beneficiaries you've had all along and concentrate on someone *else* who needs you more than they do right now.

This person is yourself.

Listen to your own pain (and your own pleasure). At the moment, you are so hurt by your children that very few things may seem pleasurable. BUT if you can learn to let go of your expectations of undying gratitude from your kids, if you can pat yourself on the back for being the best kind of mom there is — one who helps her kids grow up to be adults who can fend for themselves and thus don't need her—if you can value yourself at least half as much as you value your kids (and that's just for starters), then you will be providing a model of maturity not only for your children but for all of us as well. And most of all, a model for yourself.

The way is not easy, I know. There are very few other women over fifty you can look up to. But it can be done, WAITING. Please tell me if there is anything else I can do for you.

[signature]

Dear Dr. Holmes:

Last December 3 and 4, 1993 you discussed the problems of WAITING, who at age fifty-two was depressed that her children no longer needed her. You said that since she was a person who clearly needed to be needed, she could start focusing on someone who needed her now more than her children did. You suggested that that person was herself.

I have no quarrel with your suggestions in principle. Children are not children forever and the mark of a good parent is being able to let go when the time comes. But I cannot agree with you regarding who needs her more than ever before. Asking her to focus on herself will only be encouraging a selfishness that is probably the reason for her depression in the first place. Our lives take on meaning only when we reach out to other people and focus on them instead of on ourselves.

Don't you think that her husband needs her more now than ever before and that the focus of her life could once again shift from managing the children to concentrating on her husband who would welcome her fussing over him once more the way she used to before the children came? She could again give him the attention he deserves, making him special meals she might have been too busy to prepare when the children were younger, rekindling the romance that was put aside when the demands of career and child rearing were just too much. Now is that time to have it all back. There is a song entitled " Love is lovelier the second time around." That is so true and marital life is where you will find many models for the happily mature woman you decry we are in such need of.

I am a woman also in my fifties so I know what I am talking about. My husband and I were very busy in the first thirty years of married life and had no time to do the kind of things we used to do when we were single. We were not as well off as we are now, but we had fun. We had romance. When the children came and the demands of the business increased, romance had to take a back seat. Now that our children are grown, we can concentrate on each other once more.

Our children are all professionals. Our two boys are doctors, one girl is a nurse and another a pharmacist.

There is nothing that gives my husband and me more pleasure than holding hands after our children visit us on Sunday afternoons. We now have nine grandchildren, with another due in March, and they also give us many hours of happiness. But I would not be as happy if I did not have my husband by my side, loving, supporting and encouraging me. I would not be the person I am now. I am very happy with my life. I enjoy my work and my friends but I wouldn't have enjoyed them as much if my husband were not there to encourage me, even including having outside interests.

I am contented and serene, qualities to which women my age and WAITING'S are entitled. Husbands are entitled to attain these qualities and WAITING's husband can help her too if she would only give him the chance.

That means she will now have to pay more attention to him than to her children. Before it was they that needed her; now it is he. It isn't easy being a fiftyish man in the Nineties, and head of a family that seems to continually grow. If WAITING pays more attention to her husband, she will find him more than willing to give her the attention she needs. In a way she is paying attention to herself, because making him happy is really making both of them happy.

Thank you very much, Dr. Holmes, for giving me the opportunity to share what life in the fifties can be. There is too much negativism about women our age and I hope this letter will dispel that. I hope this letter helps people realize that not all fifty-year-olds are "over the hill."

I admit that it was not always as easy as it is now. My husband was no saint then, in the early years, though he has more than made up for it now. There were many times I cried myself to sleep at night. He had more affairs than I care to count, but they were not with anyone who mattered and in the end he always came home to me. It wasn't always easy taking him back, especially when the affair was carried on so scandalously that other people couldn't help but notice. But I am glad I didn't throw him out as I was tempted to do. Otherwise, who

116

would I have now? That is why I urge WAITING to pay attention to her husband before it is too late. Women in their fifties can still be beautiful if they look after themselves, but not in such a way as to appeal to other men. Our beauty now is more a beauty from within, that comes from a life of service to others. Men, on the other hand, are different. They can always find other women to be attracted to them so we wives must always be alert.

In case any of your readers are wondering about our sex life, my husband and I are enjoying it more now than we ever did before. It is not so much the amount of activity nor the intensity of it. For me, it is more the knowledge that at least he is mine and will no longer dally with other women. Of course it is not as passionate as it used to be in our first year of marriage before the children and the other women took their toll, but it is still there, still as much of a comfort and reassurance as it used to be.

Besides, as we get older, I find we need the physical aspect of sex less and less. We become more like brother and sister instead of man and wife. This is what the relationship of couples in their fifties becomes and the sooner people accept it, the better it will be, even for their children.

Tell WAITING not to neglect her husband and she will find untold treasures and delights. It is said that what you sow, so also shall you reap. The more she concentrates on him, the better; the more positive she is about his dreams, efforts and achievements, the kinder and more encouraging he will be to her. The more moral support she gives him for all his doubts and failures, the stronger he will be for her. After all is said and done, whom are we left to be with anyway? No one but the man we promised to "love, honor, and obey till death do us part."

My husband may not always behave like the man of my dreams. He forgets birthdays and anniversaries and still expects warm meals when he comes home late from work. But he is still my husband and nobody else's. There is no knowledge more comforting than that.

Thank you, Dr. Holmes, for giving me the opportunity to share my views. You don't have to answer this letter since I have no problem I want solved anyway.

A HAPPILY MARRIED WOMAN

Dear HMW (HAPPILY MARRIED WOMAN):

I had mixed feelings reading your letter. On the one hand, I was grateful for your articulating the stance of a particular kind of woman over fifty. She is the kind who perceives herself to have a happy and successful relationship with her husband. On the other hand, I was quite startled by your presumption that what worked for you would automatically work for everyone else, or might even be something everyone else would aspire for.

I hope I do not come across as being too hard on you. I mean what I say about you taking the time and trouble to honestly share your feelings with us. Some people would consider you the silent majority and I am glad that, through your efforts, we know a little bit more about that majority's (perceived) achievements and aspirations.

Since you spoke eloquently for your case, I would like to play devil's advocate and speak for the other silent majority, i.e., women who by choice or force of circumstance (the never married or those whose husbands are no longer a part of their lives through divorce, separation or death). This other majority is silent because they are painfully aware that our culture considers them as "failures" since they are "unlucky" enough to be single in their later years.

Surprisingly enough, however, this is not how the women see themselves. On the contrary, they consider themselves very lucky not to have a man in their lives at this time. Sometimes this comes as an utter surprise even to them. I have had many women who, after a year or two of grieving, discovered not only that life moved on, but moved in ways they never dreamed possible. Without a man to cater to or cajole, they were able to do so much more in and for their lives. Without a man to have to coordinate schedules and finances with, they found themselves having more time, energy and money on their hands to do what they pleased, when they pleased and with whom they pleased.

I am talking particularly about women whose husbands have left them to "find themselves" (which is usually merely a euphemism the men used for leaving their wives for another woman because they hoped the other interpretation would mean they would pay less). These women were nervous wrecks way before they broke up with their husbands although many of them did a good job of hiding their condition. They knew their husbands had a particular other woman (or was vulnerable to most any other woman) and were thus constantly on the lookout wondering if this little cutie or that attractive stranger would be it (the rival who would finally take their husbands away). Surely, this is not the most serene way to live one's life.

Some of these women did the leaving instead of waiting to be left. They decided life was too short to live as though constantly on the edge like that, especially if someone else was benefiting from it and not them. Other women, of course, kept on till the bitter end, thinking traditional mores and beliefs would vindicate them (as in "kay haba-haba ng prusisyon, sa simbahan din duduling," which, loosely translated, means "no matter how often he strays, your husband will always come back to you." These women hung on by the skin of their teeth, only to find out that patience, tears, prayers and "kindness" didn't really pay off: either their husbands left them anyway or they stayed because nobody else would put up with their selfish, childish ways the way their wives did.

Those women whose husbands left were broken-hearted at first. But after getting over the embarrassment and anger and real pain of being separated women and the pain of being left by the men they thought would be by their side forever, these women found to their utter delight that life without the men was so much more peaceful and serene. For one thing, they didn't have to constantly be beautiful. They could be beautiful only when they wanted to be. They could wear the styles they liked in the colors they wanted. They could laugh as loudly and as raucously as they wanted without fearing their husbands would find them unfeminine. An even bigger bonus for them was discovering that other women were kind, smart, wonder-

119

ful, interesting and worth knowing. They found they could be real friends with them, an impossible situation when their husbands looked at everyone else as fair game and they thus had to keep other women at arm's length to "protect their interests."

And then again there were some women who stayed with their husbands *physically* but emotionally divorced themselves from them. Usually, it was because being emotionally close to their husbands was too draining or too painful. Either their husbands criticized them viciously, fooled around constantly or needed them too intensely. So these women found a life of their own despite staying in the marriage. This, I believe, is what WAITING chose to do and that is why I did not, as you so constantly suggested, demand that she pay attention to her husband more.

WAITING was a woman who was thinking of killing herself, for Chrissake ! ! If she had a husband who really mattered to her, do you think she would've gone to pieces merely because her children did what children their ages were supposed to do?! ! ? If she had a husband from whom she was not divorced emotionally, don't you think she would've gone to him for solace and support instead of writing to me about it? To suggest she look to her relationship with him as her mainstay is like rubbing salt over the wound.

I know, I know, she said he was a "good husband." But there's good and there's *good*. The first is a "ho-hum-for-lack-of-a-better-word-good" and the second is a "*damn*-good !-good." Her husband was definitely the first kind of good.

It seems fifty is as good a time as any to do what you want with (or without) whomever you want, yes, yes, even for the most guilt-ridden and other-centered mother and wife among us. All things being equal, she would've raised her kids, paid her dues, landed that contract, earned her spurs. Her debts to society are usually all paid off by then too.

It seems to me that one of the greatest joys about being fifty is not having to listen to other people's shoulds and shouldn'ts.

It seems to me that at fifty one can accept more graciously, but not defeatist-ly, what one can and cannot do, mainly because one knows who one is by this time. You don't need a man to do that, though he can, of course, be a welcome diversion. But what is even more welcome is knowing you can do it all on your own if you want to. You do not need to do it on your own and I am glad for you. But I am also glad that other women do not feel the necessity to have a man just because women like you have one.

Dear Dr. Holmes:

Like WAITING and "A HAPPILY MARRIED WOMAN" (can she really be happy with a life that sounds no more than death warmed over?), I too am a woman in my fifties, although many people would be surprised to hear that. You are the first person I've told my real age to in many, many years. Most people think I am only thirty-eight and I do not correct them. I would've preferred that they think I'm only twenty-three, which is how I feel inside, but there are limits to how far you can stretch the truth.

My boyfriend is thirty-five. He thinks going out with "an older woman" is pretty cool but I don't know how he would feel if he finds out I am fifteen years older instead of only three. Will he get disgusted? Will he lose his erection? Will he abandon me at the time I need him most? Every day I am in constant fear that he will find out, but so far I've been lucky.

I think about telling him the truth but good sense always prevails. Who in his right mind would go out with a fifty-year-old? Not anyone who could go out with someone younger, I'll bet. My boyfriend teases me constantly about our age difference (if he only knew!). He cannot help constantly bringing it up because he thinks it's so "modern." If I were really only thirty-eight, I would too.

You may wonder how I have been able to get away with all this for so long! I work hard at it. I work out at the gym at least three hours a day. I lift weights, do aerobics training and regularly get a massage and a facial. I take care of my body so it doesn't betray me. But sometimes I wonder how long I can keep this up. I have had cosmetic surgery twice and will do so again when necessary. I am also taking hormone replacement therapy.

It's funny, isn't it? HAPPILY MARRIED WOMAN pities WAITING and I pity her, but now I wonder whether she has the better life, after all. I long for a man with whom I need not hide my age, but where can I find him?

JOAN

Dear JOAN:

You are obviously a bright woman to have been able to character-
ize so accurately the relationship among WAITING, HAPPILY
MARRIED, and you— three women in their fifties. Or to assess
HAPPILY MARRIED's marriage so sharply (albeit quite accurately).

Your brightness is one of the reasons I decry your lack of faith in
men.

I know, I know. A lot of them are selfish and inconsiderate. Some
of them may even act like assholes. But every now and then you come
across one who is genuine and really worth knowing. I doubt your
present boyfriend falls in this category. But just because he doesn't,
doesn't mean others can't.

If you feel he cannot handle the real, as opposed to the mythical
age difference between the two of you, why hang around him at all?
Life is too short to constantly have to hide one of the most basic
things about who you are. There are other men around who would
love to be with a woman in her fifties. Wouldn't it be far smarter to
hang around such men? . . . Unless you are a rabid agist yourself and,
like Groucho Marx who didn't want to join any club that would
accept him as a member, find such men absolutely batty and not
worth your time. Such agists are also masochists, of course, constantly
choosing men who would demean them by their jokes and actions,
even if you have the excuse that he doesn't know better. But you
know better, you see, and it is a shame for someone who loves men
to shortchange herself by being with someone who doesn't want a
woman quite like her. I kid you not. There are many, many men out
there who would jump at the chance to go out with a woman your
age. I will have you know that this is not a meaningless pep talk. If
you wish to know more about women healthily and happily in love
and lust at fifty and beyond, please write me again as I am quite fond
of this topic.

Your brightness is also the reason I decry your lack of faith in
yourself. I agree with you that looking good is important, but,
JOAN, three hours in a gym every day? Not to mention facials,

cosmetic surgery, massages and hormone replacement therapy? All these things have their place, of course. Frankly, if you'd even so much as hint at indulging in endeavors other than looking good, I wouldn't feel so *sayang* (hesitant) you were wasting your entire life on something as superficial as looks when you so obviously have the brains, the energy, and the heart for so many other things, but as it is....

Gloria Steinem, when complimented that she didn't look like she was really forty, said: "Maybe this is what really forty looks like."

It is women like you who can show us how being fifty really looks, feels and tastes. Women like you can show us what being fifty really means. Definitely, it means more than feeling empty because the kids have left the nest or hanging on to an old geezer just because you don't want to end up alone. Being fifty isn't the same as being twenty-three, but it can be just as exciting, just as promising, and certainly just as fulfilling.

Even as I write this, I am conscious that some of you may think I am merely mouthing empty, politically correct but hardly accurate statements. That is only because all of us have been trained to fear middle age, especially middle-aged women who do not have the same social cache as middle-aged men or even younger women, for that matter. But many of these prejudices about "older women" are just that—prejudices based on faulty perceptions and even more faulty reasoning. These myths, fortunately, are not written in stone and so can be changed, ever so slowly and sometimes not steadily, but changed nonetheless. It is women like you who can bring about these changes, who can prove not by words but by their lives, that being fifty doesn't mean settling for second best or apologizing for who or what you are. How about it?

In the Middle of the Road to Eternity

Marra PL. Lanot

Twenty-five times hair rearranged me
though no silver streak grew
on my head, only the natural
strands of sienna, burgundy, red
and gold, peeping through my crown
of black, colors I inherited
from my great-grandmother,
so for twenty-five years you've hardly
noticed a wrinkle here and there
or how my sweetness melted in
the clean cupboards
the shining tiles
the laundered socks and shirts
the disinfected toilet bowl
and all that relive the times
I enjoyed the band and the march
and I had to trot home before dark.

But then I've learned to waltz
the innocence of my mother
through fragrant corn and watermelon,
tracing the intricate pattern of the fields,
careful not to fall into the puddle
and to remember the tunes my mother,
sweet to her young and wise
to men's wiles, taught me.

And I discovered rubato and syncopation
and fugue and contrapuntal,
blending reggae and the blues,
rock and *kundiman,*
the freedom of lambada and swing,
and it was never the same again.

Thus we have weathered
desert storms, earthquakes,
the El Niño heat wave,
volcanic ash and others
you never imagined were threats
worse than my mother's gaze,

and now, nearing our silver years,
we're in the middle
of the road to eternity
on a dance floor where dancers
go around in circles
and change partners
and you may always pray
as sweet as I was I stay.

MIDLIFE AMONG THE PEOPLE

CAROLINA S. MALAY

ORGANIZED, mundane Capricorn that I am, I have never been able to predict the twists and turns, the smooth flows and the turbulences of my life.

During my last semester in college, panicking at the prospect of having to make my own way in life soon, I vowed not to become a teacher, nor a journalist, like my parents. Six months later, I was working in a newspaper in the morning and teaching in the afternoon (and getting paid P160 for everything).

Visiting forbidden China in 1964, depressed by the dim light bulbs and overwhelmed by the grey-blue crowds that had milled around us for days, I consoled myself by playing a bit of Chopin on the grand piano in Shanghai's great exhibition hall. Five years later, I was to become an earnest student of revolution according to Mao.

SO IT WAS with midlife. I just slid into it: no fuss, no tears, no hot flashes. My childbearing years came to an end after a short period of uneventful decline, and that was that.

At the time, I was being held in maximum-security detention in Fort Bonifacio. Maybe that partly explains the psychological equanimity that saw me over the hump. Being isolated from almost everyone Satur and I knew, I had little opportunity for the surreptitious comparisons that I suppose one inevitably makes between oneself and one's contemporaries. And, perhaps more tellingly, between oneself and the young women within the orbit of one's husband.

Being in the underground for the preceding eighteen years prepared me, I think, for middle age.

In fact, by the *masa*'s reckoning, I was already middle-aged at the time, in my early thirties. At least I was no longer young.

Most of the activists who had gone underground, when martial law was declared, were in their late teens. The senior cadres were in their early twenties. Most went off to the countryside, armed with little more than a set of acupuncture needles and the red flags of revolution waving gloriously in their hearts.

In the urban underground, manning the mimeograph machines and desperately writing poetry, were an assortment of physicists, litterateurs, theologists and such, no longer young.

REFLECTING NOW on what midlife means for the ordinary Filipinos whose lives we shared, I realize that the idea just does not exist. I never heard anyone talk about it. There's no word for it. No one seemed to think about it, much less be bothered by it.

Unlike the upper social strata that can afford the night creams, exercise classes, and girdles, that prolong the appearance of youth, most women actually welcome the onset of menopause.

Aside from being freed from so much periodic bother with one's personal hygiene (store-bought conveniences are expensive), the big bonus is liberation from the fear of becoming pregnant again.

Being completely absorbed by the natural life cycle means, for most women of childbearing age, up to forty or more years of hard

128

work at home — especially if female children aren't produced early enough to help with washing, cooking, fetching water, chopping wood, starching the curtains, serving the family's guests. Don't wonder, then, at the buckets of tears that mothers shed when a daughter gets married: they cry as much for themselves as for the young bride — prettied up as she will never ever be again — uncaring that burdens already lie ahead.

Rather than midlife, it is the accession to adulthood that the *masa* discern as a genuine, marked turning point.

Adulthood means assuming responsibility for others.

"Hindi na bata," they say of a lad who takes care of his younger siblings.

"Bata pa kasi" is the apologetic explanation for the fourteen-year-old child-bride playing *piko* with her firstborn astride her waist.

The point of reference is *bata*: one is either young or not young. The Tagalog language has no specific term, as in English, for "adult." *Matanda* means "old," "aged," and can only mean "adult" when directly counterposed to *bata*, in *"sa* children's party *sa Pilipinas, mas maraming matanda kaysa bata."*

Magulang, on the other hand, means "mature," as in timber that is *magulang*, or an *isip* that is *magulang*. It also means, as we know, "parent" and "to be shrewd." But then the word essentially expresses a value judgment on the individual, regardless of age. It doesn't express status.

More than being a question of physical age or legal status, the true meaning of adulthood lies in the assumption of social responsibility.

It's not just being responsible for oneself — earning one's keep and staying out of trouble, basically. As long as one is being fed and sheltered by the grace of one's family, or worse, family time is spent worrying about one/ one's friends/ the girl one is courting/ the man one is seeing, one can't begin to be considered an adult. One could be fifty-five or thirty, but still *"isip bata," "iresponsable."* Decisions one makes are subject to the scrutiny and consent of the true adults.

But to be a true adult, one must not only be answerable for one's own needs and decisions. One must also assume responsibility for others. Thus, the ones who contribute substantially to the family income gain the status of true adulthood and have the right to fully participate in decision-making. Also, the *ate* or *kuya* who supports the schooling of younger siblings.

Naturally, as soon as a young person gets married and starts an independent family *(bumubukod)*, thus assuming responsibility for the new social unit, he or she is considered a true adult even in teen age.

At the very least, any decision that one makes for oneself as an adult is honored by the rest of the group. This could include such things as joining the New People's Army, trying one's luck in the big city, bringing home a wife, buying a hand tractor, or applying for a job abroad.

There are, however, limitations on adulthood. For one, women aren't generally supposed to make independent decisions for themselves. Also, poverty limits one's capacity to decide.

Women who are poor bear a daily burden of family responsibilities and should therefore enjoy full adulthood. But as long as husbands or elder sons or even elder sons-in-law are around, their approval is solicited, though not necessary.

I remember Sioning, weeping bitterly as her fingers wove a buri mat. Her father and mother lay side by side in one corner of the small hut, trying not to open their eyes because of pain, "like having sand inside your eyelids." Sioning's husband had no land of his own but worked for others lucky enough to have a place to till. She herself had been gleaning in the fields that morning, stripping grains from the ricestalks that the harvesters, her cousins, had let fall on the dry ground. A half-ganta of rice was what she got for her efforts. Sioning had no brother, and her two sisters had, like her, married poor. She felt she didn't have the right to spend from the family's meager earnings in order to take the two old people to the doctor and buy whatever medication might be prescribed. *"Ang hirap maging babae,"* she lamented. Being a woman, Sioning just couldn't make that major decision by herself, whereas a man would have gone

130

right ahead, although he might inform her about his decision before actually carrying it out.

Another limitation is that even as an adult one is not supposed to make independent decisions that "put the family to shame." Even in the urban, upper-middle-class setting, for instance, many young adults with their own jobs have to work out schemes for living away from their parents. (Unless, of course, the family home is not in Metro Manila.) In the United States, parents expect their children to leave home after the age of eighteen or twenty-one at the latest. Filipino parents won't hear of their children leaving home. They'll remodel your room, let you have your own key to the house, lay out your favorite food on the table, not complain if you give little or no money as your share of the household expenses. The only thing they don't want to do is to confront ever-inquisitive relatives, neighbors, and friends who will probably conclude that you and your parents don't get along, if you insist on moving out to a place of your own.

ASSUMPTION of family responsibilities is a voluntary obligation that allows an individual, particularly a male, to enjoy adult status in the traditional Filipino family.

People who decided to join the revolutionary struggle tore away from this traditional concept of responsibility for others as familial obligation. They talked instead of a *social* obligation, of assuming responsibility for others in the larger society, outside the immediate family and the clan or even the tribe (Kapampangan, Bisaya, Waray, Aeta, Ilukano, Kalinga, whatever). It meant leaving the family behind, with its corresponding obligations and also the security and indulgences it provides.

I myself was in my early thirties and living semi-independently when the "radical rupture" came, so it wasn't the same case as teenagers dropping out of school to go to the hills.

Still, life in the underground after some time settled down to an outward routine mimicking the everyday life of the people around us. We even dared to start a family. But, with Satur's arrest, our family was forcibly broken up.

That painful episode, paradoxically, was to be the beginning of a long period of full-time service to the revolutionary movement. Then, in my mid-thirties, I began my second blooming, a new phase in which, prevented from being a wife and mother, I could freely respond to the call of distant *tambuli*. There was so much to be done, and it was exhilarating to be a part of it.

But the physical effort required made me acutely conscious of the age gap between me and my comrades. Panting and needing to rest every twenty minutes, I would be so ashamed of my petty bourgeois background that was delaying everyone else on the mountain trail. Then I would think: why compared to these boys' mothers, many of whom were younger than me, there was really not very much to be ashamed of. The grudging realization of my limited and diminishing physical capacity, forced upon me by those punishing treks, told me early enough that middle age had come.

Shortly after turning forty, I found that being more confident in my judgment had come with age. I didn't feel so tentative anymore in expressing an opinion on matters I felt knowledgeable about. In the movement where outstanding individuals had become senior cadres by their mid-twenties, old people like me were rare enough and listened to, anytime they cared to talk.

IF THE assumption of family and/or social responsibility is what being a Filipino adult means, then midlife should mark the start of entry into old age, when one becomes *matanda* — not just physically old but more significantly, full of memories *(natatandaan)* and lessons learned *(nagtatanda)*.

It seems to me that we Filipinos find less to agonize about in midlife than Westerners do, at least to judge from a recurring theme of middle-class American literature. One factor, certainly, is the obsession with youthfulness and therefore the reluctance, in the middle years, to accept the fact of physical decline.

On another level, the angst might have something to do with the notion that one's adulthood is rightly spent in the pursuit of individual goals. Midlife is then marked by a reappraisal of these goals and one's performance in trying to attain them. I don't know if most persons, that is to say, the *masa*, in real-life America really do go through such a phase, or does it happen only in the pages of *The New Yorker*? If they do, is the process really as agonizing?

IT JUST SO HAPPENED that socialist regimes in Europe collapsed during the two years and three months I spent in military detention. And so I did go through a sort of midlife crisis anyway, as I reviewed how my life and my goals had turned out after all these years.

The time, place, and circumstances conspired to facilitate a kind of prolonged meditation on what it all meant to me as a person and as a Filipino revolutionary. There was time to read and take notes, to look deeply within myself while poking about in our tiny garden, to watch ideas take shape or self-destruct while bouncing them off my partner's ideological armor.

From that period of self-examination emerged a reaffirmation and stronger sense of the basic beliefs that made me join the struggle in the first place: that the masses of the people possess a deeper wisdom than we are able to anticipate; that working-class solidarity transcends all other bonds; that change is inevitable, it is possible to intervene in the process of change, and that, moreover, history always moves forward even when it seems to be going backward; that while their material needs are met and anticipated, human beings must also feel a higher kind of well-being, *magaan ang loob*, in order to be happy.

STEPPING OUT of prison and finding my place again in civil society after nearly twenty years, even more do I like this country and its gutsy people. I keep making mental comparisons with the Sixties, and note how much larger the nationalist constituency has become; how much more the basic masses and their organizations are making their presence felt; how decent, progressive-minded individuals have begun to be recognized as leaders in communities all over the country.

These developments, together with all the happy memories and sad lessons crowded together in my head, tell me that the long years of struggle have produced something worthwhile, solid ground to go forward on.

I do not at all share the pessimism of those who denounce the so-called indifference to social concerns of today's young people, particularly the students at the University of the Philippines. Having taught there for the past two semesters, I can say that, at the minimum, they are probably not worse than the First Quarter Storm generation, or my own UP generation, for that matter. Most are reasonably intelligent, responsive, and anxious for the future of our society. On the other hand, I find that books are less of an influence than movies and TV, but despite that their Americanization is more superficial than ours. Definitely, what I've seen of these young people assures me that we're going to be all right.

It's crucial, though, for us the incumbent generation to pose the right challenge to them and not to give up on our dreams. Nor on ourselves.

Journey and Arrival

Asuncion David Maramba

WHAT IS the object that best represents you at this stage of your life? the seminar facilitator asked. It was a simple question, but it made a lot of sense. For a good symbol is capable of instantly shedding peripheral details and distilling essence.

For a while, I played around with "a question mark," which could reveal that I was confused or curious. But that would be only half the picture because I was also clear and clear-headed about certain matters. Finally, I struck on an object that embraced the paradox of searching on the one hand, and finding on the other.

"I am a key," I said at the seminar, as I held out the key to the master bedroom in my home. "I feel like a key because I am still opening doors, questioning a number of things, and searching for answers more assiduously than ever before. But like a key I have already ' unlocked a couple of mysteries and arrived at the end of some of my seeking."

That's it. Midlife for me is both journey and arrival, search and discovery, confusion and clarity,question and answer.What I have already found and what I am still seeking are the two sides of a delicate question that must even out. Too much questioning and this midlife of mine becomes existential *angst*. And I get the feeling that I have never been so insecure. On the other hand, realization, like God unfolding, and a senseless world making some sense, have dawned on me, sometimes slowly, like a tune, or swiftly, like an epiphany. Then I feel I have never been so secure.

What have I found? What I have "found" fall into three groups. The first has always been there; I've just taken it for granted. The second consists of accumulated treasures that midlifers, having lived longer, can claim. The third consists of "new" discoveries.

Of the first group, it was upon midlife that I began never to take anything for granted — not my husband, my children, my friends, my eyesight, my home. I thanked my husband for the house he built us three years ago, something I never did for the previous houses. I thank God at every turn because I can watch the first rains of the season or walk out to the garden and see my plants and flowers (even the artificial ones in the house!).

I found that friends are precious, where before they walked in and out of my life without event. Warmth was never, to my regret, one of my strong points. I used to keep a distance; I shunned intimacy as a breeder of contempt, except for a few very special friends who never gossiped, who were never catty or silly. Chitchat was a waste of time. I'm good for only an hour of it and after that it's yawn, unless the conversation moves on to genuine talk.

What a heartwarming discovery to find out that despite betrayals and deceit aplenty in this planet,there are more than enough good friends to go around for a lifetime. I mourn when friends are lost or drift away, casualties of misunderstanding, distance,or death.

For the past years, I have cultivated new friends and renewed old ones, both individuals and groups, neighborhood friends, friends from organizations past and present, fellow teachers in every school where I have taught, writer friends, former students (who now call me by my nickname).

And former schoolmates — that great reservoir of friends. The dozen or so that "remain" of our Maryknoll high school class get together only once in a blue moon, but when we do it's with a closeness that we didn't have way back in school when we saw each other every day. Now we bare our souls and genuinely feel for each other.

Theresian friends have increased upwards and downwards to include batches that graduated years before or after me, all bunched together as midlifers in their forties, fifties, sixties, indulging in the good old days, among other things.

For midlifers look backward. Why do you think homecomings are filled with midlifers? Unbelievable, but after snubbing homecomings for two decades, we "come home." As we sing the good old college song, we hide the quiver on our lips and a tear drops. School is now "alma mater," now a term of endearment, layered with unforgettable associations about "the best years of our lives," permeated with sentiment and gratitude so lately felt. Homecomings warm the heart and in this cold world what's left to warm the heart but newfound rites of friendship? Who cares if you're rich or poor, separated, single, happy, or unhappy? Who dares call homecomings "escape"? Every midlifer will tell you it's a renewal. That's no illusion.

But so be it, if you insist. Nostalgia begins at midlife and may be a sign of old age. But that's only because by midlife we have stored a lode of memories: bitter-sweet, mostly sweet, mysteriously rendered thus by the passage of time that leaves the past with a patina of beauty and the most poignant of sentiments; memories that now rise unbidden with a passing scene, a fragrance, a tune, an object, a mood, a road, a person, a photograph. I understand Proust's *Remembrance of Things Past* perfectly.

It was at midlife that I sat down for hours and put together albums of my children's photographs from birth to grade school

137

graduation, from high school to college graduation, and thenceforth to weddings. I turned over their albums to each of them as they left home. Now I have made albums for myself — a record of our babies growing up and away. I've sworn those albums are the first things I'll save in case of fire. Hoarding memories? Maybe.

It was at midlife that a childhood inextricably linked with relatives and the old hometown impinged itself upon my consciousness. I say "itself" because childhood-relatives-hometown flow into each other such that they seem to be but one. "Idyllic" is the only word that comes close to the experience.

There's a strain of *promdi* (from the province) in our blood. Four out of five of us have a hometown tucked away in our childhood, a *lolo,* a *lola,* and a string of *tios* and *tias* and cousins and childhood playmates firmly fixed in the memory, and an ancestral house whose every corner and room held endless charms for us. Enthralled, I sat at the foot of *Lola* reclining in her *butaka,* chewing her *nga-nga* and telling stories of Juan Tamad. Enthralled, I walked through her garden, sniffing sampaguitas, *kampupot,* jasmine — not too close, she warned, lest the insects get into my nose.

My mother thinks the first thing I'll do when she dies is sell the one small piece of farmland she gave me. She's wrong. Unknown to her (and to me when it was happening), I bonded with such things as a rice field, a picnic in a coconut grove, burning leaves, and various smells of the earth. Such childhood bonds are hard to break.

I bonded, too, with folk religion. Living for three years right across the church in Sta. Cruz, Laguna, during the Japanese time, I couldn't help soaking in the moods of the liturgical seasons. I knew when it was Sanctus, when it was Consecration, when Angelus, when a baby was being baptized, a couple being wed, first-class or second-class, when it was Lent, Easter, Christmas — all because the church bells knew how to lament and how to rejoice. Years later, folk religion would sometimes succeed where "new" spiritualities would falter.

But summer siesta time without the siesta was the best time of all. The siesta hour, which stretched to merienda time, meant lazing in the porch, playing house, playing store, and waiting for the vendors to pass by. Those lazy afternoons were the zenith of idleness. I'm glad I had them.

I bonded with my hometown then and forever, even if, alas, its landscape was swept away by Liberation and by every generational change thereafter. The old hometown lives only in my memory.

But apart from the Pinay and *promdi* strains in my veins, my education has been decidedly Western. I do not apologize for it or for the inevitable inculturation.

Because of that education and the period of Philippine history in which I was born, and because every midlifer is at a certain time a "middle generation" standing in the center of two generations, one of my prized possessions is an incomparable historical-cultural deposit accumulated with every passing generation and continually growing as it enters the next. Modesty aside, I feel very rich with the cultural heritages behind me and before me. The feeling is one of the pinnacles of midlife. I have generously written about this cultural legacy as a motif in my life.

I have lived through at least four historical periods: the Commonwealth, Wartime, Liberation, and the Nationalist Period (from the late Sixties, that is). I have tasted or absorbed four cultures: traces of the Spanish (for culture has a way of trailing along with the new one), the American, the European, the Filipino. I have possessed little of the rest of Asia, but I'm getting there.

Personally, I do not understand the fuss over the layering of cultures. Cultures have a way of blending into each other imperceptibly. I have had no problem about finding and managing a Filipino identity in the midst of all manner of inculturation. What's more, this cultural legacy continues to grow, ever renewing, ever refining. Old is new.

BUT MIDLIFERS look forward too. We are not about to sit in rocking chairs. Even school friends held by a common past that could enchant and petrify us have eyes fixed firmly on the present and the future. The St. Theresa's Alumnae Association and Teresa

139

Makabayan may chat at merienda, lunch, and supper and go on out-of- town trips, but meetings are serious business where we try to keep attuned to what's happening at large and try to change what can be changed.

The decisively forward-looking character of our batch of midlifers owes itself to a historical event. I am of course speaking for myself but it is possible that a lot of my contemporaries feel the same way. We may not have known it then but the shot in the tarmac on August 21,1983 that felled Ninoy Aquino lodged in our brains and unwound with the rest of the country.

While other midlife experiences like arthritis and anxiety may be common to "all," August 21, 1983 to February 25, 1986 is distinctly ours. Touching us at midlife, that brief historical stretch has determined what we have turned out to be. Because of it, we may be different from midlifers past and future — a case of a historical event shaping people's lives. Our political awakening is a historical phenomenon with which midlifers in my generation can identify.

To me personally, this epiphany has been two-pronged. It constitutes two of my "new" and most significant "finds" in midlife: I picked up my writing again and I "discovered" my citizenship.

In 1982, I toyed with the idea of writing again. While I have been forever-teacher,I have only been a sometime-writer. Mine was not a career shift but a repeat of something that lay in hiatus for more than fifteen years while the children were growing up. Mine was not a studied decision in which I said to myself, now look here, Sony, get out and write again.

As I surveyed my prospects, I was intimidated by an arena of first-rate writers belonging to the generation after me, many of them my star students at St. Theresa's College Manila and St.Scholastica's College. Besides, my writing, or what was left of it, was rust. How could this late starter of a golden girl break through if she didn't have a "name" and how could she get a "name" if nobody gave her a break?

I was twiddling with the key to write or not to write again. Ninoy's death turned that key for me. On impulse, I submitted "A Call to

Closet Nationalists" to *Mr.and Ms.* I slipped into the alternative press. You might say I was off to a late start, but one that stretched steadily through eight years with succeeding or simultaneous columns: "On Living" in *Veritas* from April 1-7, 1984 to its last issue of May 14-20, 1987; "Humanly Speaking" in the *Manila Chronicle* from August 3, 1986 to March 25,1991; "The Changing Church" in the *Manila Digest* (formerly *C'or Manila*) from January 1989 to October 1990. I also edited two books on Ninoy Aquino and the EDSA Revolution and picked up a couple of writing awards along the way.

Simultaneously, Ninoy's death unlocked my newfound citizenship. I began to be conscious that I am Filipino. By grade school, what a little American I had become, thanks to the warm American nuns at Maryknoll and the handsome American Jesuits at the Ateneo. My generation succumbed to America's attractions with the greatest of ease and got introduced to the barn before getting to know the nipa hut. College, which brought European culture into my life, was the final flourish to the Western tradition in which I and my generation were almost totally immersed. Except for Maytime in *Lola*'s house and the blessed wartime stint in Laguna, there was little that was Filipino in me except my complexion. Only into my forties, during the First Quarter Storm when I visited some activist students in a police precinct, was I rudely reminded that "*hoy*," you are a Filipino."

Till then I was politically the blandest and most apathetic of citizens. Nationalism and citizenship were but words in the dictionary. "What happened to you?" my friends asked when I wrote that "Call to Closet Nationalists." I guess I must have been my first closet nationalist who came out of the closet.

It was not in my youth that I marched for a cause and attended clandestine meetings. It was at midlife. It was not in my youth that I joined rallies and motorcades, that I raised a fist and sang *"Bayan Ko"* (My Country). It was at midlife. It was not in my youth that I campaigned for an election and served at the polling place. It was at midlife.

To say the least, the awakening was heady at its height. I shared it

141

with a huge batch of midlifers for whom life has never been the same again — Tessie, Luz, Norma, Josie, Saling, Olive, Nene, Darle, Baby, Bessie, Pearl, Popsy, Mert, Mely, Virgie, Gina, and Precy, and a lot of others. It was a sisterhood that no other batch of midlifers can claim.

WHAT DO I still seek? Surprisingly, what I am still seeking lies in two areas that I thought I had already found.

The first area has to do with the family. I thought that with thirty years or so of mothering the children through babyhood, childhood, early schooling, adolescence, I'd be an expert. In fact, adolescence , bruited about to be the most difficult stage to handle was the most enjoyable for me. That stage was dominated by our children's friends of all ages, kinds and sizes, dropping into our parlor, singly like some secret, ardent admirer, or in hordes like our youngest son's bicycle pack. They lingered, ate, slept, planted themselves like zombies before the TV or the computer, played marathon ping-pong, and partied in the den.

My experience is crystallized in a recurrent recollection of that period. I enjoyed those young people's company so much that at the slightest excuse I struck up a conversation with them, like peers, except that my children gave me the eye to remind me that they were *their* friends, not mine and after the amenities, could I please disappear? If I breezed through the period when the kids were breaking into adolescence and out of it, shouldn't everything after that be a cinch?

Not quite. I am still picking my way through this latest stage of my children's adulthood, this "final cut" when they have not only moved out of the house but are disengaging themselves from their parents on all conceivable levels. Relationships with adult children are an entirely new ball game. It just occurred to me that there are books and books on babyhood and childhood and an avalanche on adolescence, but are there any how-to's on married children? Do experts imagine that parenting is all over when children marry and leave home? As the underrated old folks say, the job is never done.

142

The physical separation, surprisingly, is the least problematic. At a certain point, in fact, that is imperative. (I fully relish the luxury of being alone in the house when I want to be.) It's the nonphysical aspect of separation that is the greatest challenge to my mind and my heart — the realization that the children are so different, so distant, so paradoxically independent and dependent — and you can't, you mustn't, do anything because they're beyond your ken, unless they allow you to. Meddling is the bad word for it. Have detractors ever thought of *advice*?

If in my case the adage about the difficulties of bringing up adolescents has been proven inaccurate, the encounters with the never-ending intricacies of relating or dealing with adult children has been- wholly unexpected. Letting go has been easy for me. Letting be is another matter. The relationship, I figure, has to be substantially peer.

The second area of my ongoing search is even more surprising. You'd think that at this late stage I could finally be dramatic and say that I've found my God. That I'm *finding* my God is the better way of putting it.

In my childhood, He was a given, like the air around us. I lived by Him as I lived by the air without knowing it.

In my mid-twenties I encountered him, consciously, in Pacdal, Baguio. Undoubtedly, the six-month stint in the cool hills of Pacdal was a signal gift for a timid soul that needed some verve. I then *knew* He was there and ardently prayed that if everything should be inconstant about me, may my newfound awareness of Him always remain. I meant every word.

But back in the lowlands and into the distractions of living, I forgot. He receded again, not Him perhaps, but me, even as I lived a run-of-the-mill, upright life. But whether Him or me, He I think has been my staying power, the bottom line, unobstrusive, seemingly remote on His part and frankly neglectful on mine — but "there."

At midlife, past the mid-century of my life, I am again straining for a "new" spirituality, and this nth time around I need it to be meaningful, alive, integrative, quiet, intimate, powerful, liberating,

143

simple. Tall order that, with such "conditions". That's only because the life with God is the realm where words fail. Yet I suspect that it's not all that complex, for I feel that if you are bestowed one "gift," you are bestowed all.

Words that begin to deepen now are *prayer* and groping words like *mystery* which "revitalize the heart but bewilder the rest of us"; above all, "faith," the only eyes with which to "see" God. Only lately have I realized how often we unite these two words as we say after every Consecration at Mass, "Let us proclaim the mystery of faith." It is faith I seek, neither in the sense of religion (i.e. sect), nor in the sense that lurks behind such an unkind and arrogant remark as "you've lost your faith," but faith that transcends all that, understands that words falter.

"Many find what they seek in their work...; others... by transferring out to another human being...; some... to noble causes and ideologies... but the greatest number still plug into a transcendent God, that great power source...."

This is the God I seek; this, the immemorial journey of the soul that I am taking, in light and shadow, in consolation and agony. To have "found," to have "arrived," is to stop. This hide-and-seek, it seems to me, is always a finding, a movement, mostly His movement and a little of mine. At midlife this search has become urgent, at times very poignant.

Pursued or neglected, faint or aggressive, the God-search remains a constant presence amid mundane pursuits. For while the spirit would soar (and dive), midlife is also a time of great practicality when feet are firmly planted in the ground. Late midlife is the time in which I try to be kind to myself — no hurry, no need to prove myself.

The joys are simple and reachable. I take time for whimsy and for nothing in particular. I window-shop and buy a pair of shoes without hesitation. I take great pleasure in going through the closets, fixing, discarding, or just looking. I try to be faithful to my prayer time. I pause. I sit on the porch or rearrange the furniture and shift the decor around the house. I read light matter and look at pictures. I lunch with friends and I'm learning to chat.

Lately, if I've done my work or my "deed for the day," I no longer look for something else to do; the rest of the day is "mine." I avoid bad news on TV and in the papers. I "wait" for things to happen. If I get something printed in the papers once a month, I'm happy. When *Catholic Digest* reprints one of my articles, I feel flattered. I have started to watch movies again and I hope to play the piano again — as soon, that is, as I get the right pair of glasses.

My desires are everybody else's dreams — well-being, *joie de vivre,* and a measure of habitual peace. I intend to slow down, not in preparation for a full stop but as a conditioning for a slow, steady pulse that can go on beating for yet another generation. My mother is almost ninety and my father ninety-one; both are going strong. The genes are good. Most probably I'll live as long as they and finally be forced to admit that "Sony, you're now a senior citizen."

An Unmarried Woman

Imelda M. Nicolas

I MMEDIATELY upon waking up in the morning, I have gotten into the habit of reading from the book *Daily Guideposts,* described by its publisher as "spirit-lifting thoughts for every day of the year."

Coincidentally, when I was asked to contribute to this collection of essays, the vignette for the day from *Daily Guideposts* was from one Arthur Gordon, who had this to say:

> *"Today is my seventy-fifth birthday, an unyielding chronological fact that I regard with considerable amazement. How did this venerable milestone come over the horizon so soon? Seventy-five! There must be a mistake somewhere. But there isn't.*
> *"Well, never mind, I don't feel all that ancient. Perhaps this is because of an idea I borrowed from a friend some years ago. When I asked him to define old age, he said cheerfully, 'Oh, that's easy. Old age is always fifteen years older than the age*

you're at. When you're forty-five, its's sixty. When you are sixty, it's seventy-five. When you get to seventy-five, it's ninety. That way you never reach old age, because it's always receding before you.!'"

This passage struck me because perhaps it explains why I have always felt young or, at the very least, I have never felt old. I have never been conscious of my age.

In fact, when I told my bosom friend that I'm being asked to write on midlife crisis and such, he quipped, "Then your first crisis will be whether or not to admit in black and white that you are reaching the mid-century of your life. Are you ready to reveal your age? Isn't that a catastrophe of the first order? A dilemma worthy of a Margaret Mead."

I laughed because it has never occurred to me to deny my age. Of course, it helps when they say you have the "right genes." My mother died at the age of eighty-one and at her funeral, family friends would gaze with affection at the face of a woman who looked sixty.

But writing this essay has also set me thinking. Why my youthful attitude? Has my being unmarried got anything to do with it? Does it help that I do not have conventional milestones to mark the passage of time?

I am not being perverse about it, nor am I trying to make singlehood seem the ideal state of affairs. But married women naturally peg time by major turning points in their lives: their wedding day, their first child, their *bunso's* first day in school, the children's graduation from elementary, then high school, and finally college, the first wedding of a child in the family. The list is endless. Every occasion becomes a reminder of how time flies. The thought "I am getting old" keeps flashing in one's mind at every momentous event.

But not for me. "Tsk, tsk," some would say with a hint of pity in their voices, "you don't know what you're missing." That's precisely the point. I really don't know what I'm missing and I really don't care to know.

Then there is the matter of being alone most of the time, because of which I have developed the habit of introspection. I am always assessing myself and where I stand at the moment.

So far I have not reached the midlife crisis painted so vividly by Gail Sheehy in her celebrated book, *Passages*. For a lot of men and women who have struggled so hard to get where they are, so intent on building and providing for a family, the forties and the fifties become the fork in the road with the big, garish neon sign of a question mark: "Is that all there is?" or "Is this what I really wanted?"

But do not get me wrong. The life of an unmarried woman is not all violins and roses. There is always someone lurking out there — an intrepid matchmaker. The moment the person finds out that I am not married, he or she starts salivating, envisioning the image of an unmarried brother or nephew, a widowed friend, or a divorced business associate.

Actually, I find it insulting that these people should think I am incapable of having a love life without their help. In fact, the best way for me to detest someone, sight unseen, is for him to be suggested as a possible blind date or future husband.

Then there are those whose smirks, the moment they hear I am single, are just too odious to describe. "Aha!" you could hear bells ringing in their head and the wheels turning round and round in their brain, "She's either a lesbian or an easy lay. A repressed, frustrated, desiccated spinster, ready to jump into bed at the twitch of a finger." Quick and neat stereotypes, anyone?

Like almost every woman who reached her thirties without having borne a child, I had my share of anxiety attacks regarding my biological clock going tick, tock, tick, tock. "Intimations of mortality" and thoughts of "what will be left of me after I'm gone" became more intense at this age. Before the anguish became too unbearable, however, the decision was taken away from me by a hysterectomy that could not be denied.

Those are the minuses in the romance department. The pluses are many and varied. Because my relationship is not "secured" by a marriage contract, there is always the element of newness and the challenge of holding on. You know someone is sticking around, not because of a legal paper that states he should or else he could lose half of his property to someone who does not happen to be a blood relation.

The absence of a contract, of cut-and-dried rules, gives me flexibility beyond compare. Flying off to another country at a moment's notice is no big thing. No husband to ask permission from, no children to feel guilty about. I schedule my life with a freedom that is unthinkable to some women. I could indulge in activities beyond the nine-to-five working girl's timetable without any qualms, and without hesitation.

It goes a long way if your male friend has a solid sense of self, an ego that does not feel threatened by a woman of independent means and mind. But since I am attracted to men of equally strong will, a contest of wits and will is inevitable, exciting but sometimes exhausting.

AT THIS POINT, some would perhaps ask, is that why it was easier for you to become a feminist?

Surprisingly enough, this side of me did not come like the bolt of lightning that struck Saul of Tarsus on his way to Damascus. It was an evolutionary process that was so natural I did not even realize I was such.

In a way, I have to hand it to my parents for having been gender neutral when it came to rearing their five children, three boys and two girls. I never heard either my father or my mother say, "You cannot do that because you are a boy" or "because you're a girl."

They gave my sister and me the same opportunities for education. We could be whatever we wanted to be: businessperson, politician, engineer, lawyer, interior designer, architect, or pastor. They never gave the patronizing admonition that we had to prepare ourselves for our husbands or become the best women we could be for our future mates.

Even when I was nearing the age that our local argot colorfully calls "the last trip," my parents never pressured me into marriage. So their daughter was single, what was the big deal? They never made

150

me feel that they were bothered by the "stigma" of having a *"matandang dalaga."*

Serendipitously, my education had something to do too with my feminism. Both in high school and in college, the schools I attended were never into the "females only" courses. No mandatory cooking and sewing classes. No subjects were considered "too masculine" for our taste. Ateneo was teaching epistemology and ontology. So were we taught. De La Salle had logic and physics. Why not us as well?

Right after graduation, though, I found out that girls who knew all these things could be a worse deterrent to boys than body odor and bad breath. Again, I got over that quickly enough, since I realized that those who would shirk from intelligent women had single-digit IQs anyway and our conversations would be reduced to monosyllables and grunts of *"Talaga?"* I would be bored to the gills within thirty minutes, so forget about lifetime commitment.

The friends I had, both here and abroad, were never the type to panic when they had no Saturday night dates. Although we were surrounded by other girls who couldn't stop talking about their boyfriends, who would spend hours on end mouthing sweet nothings on the phone, who would always be *au courant* on the latest cosmetics and fashion, somehow we remained immune to this "girlish" virus.

In a way, the milieu I was in never made me feel discriminated against because I was a woman. The first time I encountered sexual discrimination was in the United States, of all places. I was with my Filipino male partner talking to a potential client (who happened to be a true-blue WASP—White Anglo-Saxon Protestant American) and the latter refused to acknowledge my presence. He would speak only to my partner and treat me as if I were a secretary with pretensions of being a businesswoman. He half-expected me to open my mouth only to offer "Coffee, tea, or me?" I was too much of a lady to hit him with my briefcase, which I was itching to do.

A year after graduation in the mid-Sixties, I left for the States and stayed for three years. I caught the trail of the flower children in Haight-Ashbury. But I got more than a whiff of tear gas from the

151

radical students of the US. One day, I was innocently making my way to my art history class in Columbia U, and the next day the SDS and the Weathermen (the American version of our Kabataang Makabayan) had taken over our building.

Those were the heady, earth-shaking days of America's counter-culture — the protest marches against the Vietnam War, the assassinations of Martin Luther King and Robert Kennedy, the riots in the streets of Harlem. The Women's Lib movement was strident and became known more for its bra-burning image than for the principles the women were fighting for, no thanks to the male-dominated media.

I imbibed all of these and by the time I got back to the Philippines, I was Americanized by half, with a rebellious and irreverent streak, very up front, straight to the point, with a can-do attitude.

I had some friends who had gone through the same American experience and together we launched a so-called "underground" tabloid which we dubbed, tongue-in-cheek, "Imelda's Monthly." The gang was having so much fun that as a sequel we "threatened" to come up with a magazine, this time with the monicker "Ferdie's Organ." But the Great Dictator lowered the boom on all of us. He declared martial law.

For a while, I felt it was too presumptuous to consider myself jail bait, just like my boss then, the young senator Ninoy Aquino. But by December 8, 1972, right after the assassination attempt on First Lady Imelda Marcos, I was picked up from my house at the crack of dawn by the Philippine Constabulary and thrown into Camp Crame.

I made the rounds of the camps — from Aguinaldo to Bonifacio to Crame — thus the quip that I share with many former political detainees, that I am a graduate of the ABC University. I ended up as the commander of the women's camp in Bonifacio, but in six months I was out of Marcos' jail.

Then, during the parliament of the streets, after the assassination of Ninoy Aquino, I became one of the founding officers of GABRIELA, a broad-based alliance of women who were opposed to the almost twenty years of the Marcos dictatorship. Looking back, I don't

152

believe there was any feminist agenda underlying GABRIELA then. The only things we had in common were that we were women and we all wanted the Marcoses out of our lives.

It was only after the EDSA revolution and with Cory Aquino's assumption of the presidency that I started to feel it was about time we looked after our own interests as women. As I dug deeper, the more I realized the inequality and discrimination and the marginalization and trivialization of Filipino women could be very subtle in our society but prevalent and insidious nonetheless. It could take the form of a woman farmer who is denied ownership of the land she tills because "a farmer is a man." It could mean that a woman factory worker who works side by side with a man takes home a salary that is only a third of his. A complaint by a battered wife is met by law enforcement officials with a shrug and a disclaimer, *"Away ng mag-asawa iyan. Hindi kami puwedeng makialam."* (That is a private matter between husband and wife. We cannot get involved.)

In the government, for every four male executives there is only one female boss. This is despite the fact that the majority in the bureaucracy are women and that the women in higher positions have a slightly higher educational attainment than the men.

I COULD GO on and on with the statistics but on a personal level I have reached a point in my life where I feel that it's about time I relayed to my fellow women the same sense of empowerment I have as my own woman.

Men are not the enemy. Most of the time we are our own worst foes. We have developed our own sense of limitation. We allow other people to take our own measure. We look at the world with their eyes, mainly men's. And instead of building each other up, some of us tend to claw each other down.

We should be happy when our sisters make it in this world. We know how hard the struggle has been; we have been there before. In their happiness we should see reflections of our own image and likeness. That should be reward enough.

Some of my greatest heartbreaks have been caused by women

friends. One particular crisis forced me to take a long pause and seek counseling. The counselor made me see that perhaps this was my subconscious way of saying to myself that I had overdeveloped one side of my personality, the intellectual, to the detriment of my emotional *persona*. I am too task-oriented, I forget the flesh-and-blood person behind the task. I am an efficiency freak, losing effectivity in the process. I am a card-carrying controller. Too bossy for my own good. The fire-breathing Dragon Lady in the flesh. A hyper, Type A personality to the core.

I know the counselor is right, but at midlife how do you make a turnaround? That is the challenge that faces me now, as I look forward to the almost other half of the century—as an Unmarried Woman in the prime of my life.

LETTING GO:
A WIDOW IN MIDLIFE

ALICE A. PAÑARES

RAU DIED just nine days after our eighteenth wedding anniversary. He was forty-six years old. Zeena, our daughter, was only sixteen. And I felt seventy. It wasn't right. Rau shouldn't have died so young. Only old people can die. I was not ready to be a widow.

Even then he had looked well. He did not lose weight; His appetite was good; he would talk and move about, though slowly. But he was terribly sick inside: he had a big tumor at the base of his neck and a big lump of pain in the depth of his heart. It was a pain he shared with me all throughout that year before he died. It was a pain over which I had no control.

When Rau died, I was devastated. Literally, I lost half of me. My body was testimony to that loss. Two months before, I had a mastectomy. I lost my right breast. Maybe my tumor was the accumulation of that whole year of Rau's pain, which was doubly painful for me because I could only listen, sympathize, encourage, but I couldn't take away the pain he had to undergo while doing a job he didn't want. Maybe my tumor was a carryover of a genetic defect — my mother had had the same condition years ago. Maybe midlife was catching up with me and my body was just showing signs of aging. Maybe my body was telling me what my mind refused to accept: that Rau's sickness was serious and he might die, because eleven years before, he had also had a tumor and almost died.

When I had the mastectomy, Rau and my gang of women friends reacted to it more than I did. They were worried sick for me. They were at my bedside before the operation, cheering me up. They stayed throughout the hours of surgery, keeping Rau company, and when I was wheeled out of the operating room, still groggy from the anesthesia, I could hear their voices and feel their reassuring presence beside him.

My friends knew he wouldn't have the heart to break the bad news to me, and so they stayed until I opened my eyes and mumbled, "Did they remove my breast?" They had tears in their eyes when they answered haltingly, "Yes, they did." "Oh, no," I cried, "I'd look terrible in my bathing suit! How could I swim? ... I so love to swim ... Why did the doctor take it away?" I mumbled crazily through my drowsiness. But I was looking for Rau because I knew he was more worried about me and at that moment he had enough to worry about. His eyes were bothering him, he had trouble keeping his balance, and he tired easily. He was in fact no longer well when I had the operation, but he endured sleeping on the sofa bed in my hospital room, refusing to heed my urging that he go home and rest.

Every day, my faithful women friends, my family and Rau's, my colleagues in school, and his officemates came with bouquets of flowers, boxes of pastries and chocolates, balloons, and crazy greeting cards to affirm that they loved me just the same with one breast less. It must have been hard for Rau to welcome all those visitors while he himself was not feeling well.

I had no time to mourn the loss of my right breast. A little more than a month later, Rau underwent a series of physical examinations and soon after had to check into the hospital himself. The test results were not good. He had a tumor again but this time I was not too worried because he did not change physically, unlike eleven years ago when he first became ill. He could still make it, I thought. But he did not. Three weeks later, just a day after we came home from the hospital, he died, quietly. It was so typical of him to go that way. I hardly realized he was gone.

I had truly lost half of me — my better half. Every time I faced the mirror, my body would be a grim, silent reminder that Rau was gone. The scar that remained after my right breast was removed was a long, straight minus sign stitched on my chest. In a real sense, Rau's death was the greatest subtraction of joy and love in my life. How apt the word *widow* is: without love, without joy, without him.

LOOKING BACK, I realize now that women have been the constant force sustaining me through all the emotional breaking points of my life as a widow.

Right after Rau's death, my sister, Rau's sister, his mother, and my group of women friends took over the hundred and one details that had to be attended to: calling the funeral parlor; filling up the hospital forms; notifying family, relatives, friends, officemates; writing the obituary and having it published; scheduling prayers, services, songs, and Masses; bringing an endless supply of hot food, coffee, cookies, candies; arranging flowers and keeping tabs of the Mass cards, gifts, and money given to me; and stealing me away from the endless hordes of friends who came at all hours of the day and night, so I could eat, shower and sleep. They were an efficient, tireless nucleus of workers who knew no time, for even in the loneliest hours of dawn I saw them there beside me.

On the periphery, my male friends also kept vigil, but death and grief were awkward landscapes for them. They stayed quietly in the corners of the room, ready to help, bringing in the heavy cases of soft drinks or rearranging chairs and benches, feeling helpless and lost, unable to follow me into the depths of my sorrow. But to my women friends, this was familiar territory: they knew pain and death and grief from their experience of motherhood. And so they mothered me during those endless days and nights and cupped my tears in the shelter and privacy of their embrace, taking me in as their lost child in my new widowhood.

On the tenth day, right after the ninth-day novena-Mass, I was to leave for the United States to attend a two-week summer art workshop in California. The trip, part of my sabbatical requirements, had been planned months before, when my school granted me a sabbatical. When Rau became ill, I told him I would postpone the trip until he got well or even cancel it, but he insisted that I go. "No, you must go as scheduled. I will get well and you can go on your trip." How well he chose the day he would die. He always had an exquisite sense of time, being a broadcaster, and his death was no exception. He allowed me to fulfill the novena prayers for him and still make it to the States. At first, I refused to even consider leaving, but after Zeena, my relatives and women friends insisted it would be a good break for me and I would be fulfilling what Rau wanted, I relented. I wanted to take Zeena along, but she chose to stay behind. She was graduating from high school and it would be her last year with classmates she had became so close to. I made the trip alone.

It proved to be a healing balm. For three weeks, I blotted out of my consciousness, if only momentarily, the recent nightmare of Rau's last days, his death, the wake, the burial. The relatives and old girl friends I stayed with all took me into their arms and understood, without asking for details, knowing the wounds were too raw, the memories too fresh to be recalled. They took me around, sightseeing, shopping, swimming. The brightness and newness of the California landscape, the novelty of the sights in summer, the general gaiety and warmth of the beaches, and the overwhelming bigness of everything — the food, the people, the buildings — told me that life goes on. I threw away all my black clothes and wore red. I swam and laughed and danced at the country club. We traveled endlessly; in Mexico we bought espadrilles and silver jewelry. I wanted so desperately to forget that Rau was gone. I wanted to believe he was just away for a few days and would be home when I arrived from my trip. I succeeded, for some days.

The art workshop itself was an intensive two-week course that kept me very busy listening to speakers, visiting museums, and writing a new art syllabus.

It was in the US that I was confronted with my new status: new widow, young widow. WIDOW. What a strange word. Was that me? As a joke and later a serious undertaking, my friends started introducing me to single men, recently divorced men, and widowers. I found it amusing that barely a month after Rau's death my friends were already matching me off. How could I ever look at another man again? No one could be like Rau. No one could take his place. I was married to him forever.

After three weeks, I had to go home. I was worried about how Zeena was coping with her father's death. She and I and Vicky, our reliable helper of ten years, had a tearful reunion. Zeena told me how caring her classmates and teachers had been after her dad's death and how they had gone out of their way to console her. Even her busmates had been extra kind and thoughtful. While I was gone, my sister and her two children, who lived next door, practically adopted Zeena. I was relieved to learn that she had weathered those first days well.

As Zeena busied herself later with all the gifts I had brought her from the States, I went up to the bedroom Rau and I had shared, slowly, apprehensively. I opened the door, half expecting to see him in bed, reading a book as he had been wont to do. The big bed was huge and empty. I looked around the room. Everything was the same as it had been: Rau's books, his reading glasses, his cologne. I opened our clothes closet. All his things — shirts, pants, suits, neckties — were hanging there, waiting to be used. I touched one of his shirts and brought it to my face. I could smell his cologne. Immediately, I burst into tears. I sat on the bed and sobbed into a pillow. It smelled of him. Everything in the room — the books, the magazines, even the vases and knick-knacks he had given me — reminded me of him. I felt the urge to sweep everything away, throw everything out of my sight. At the same time, I wanted to cling to

159

each item, smell it, and hold each one that Rau had owned, hoping to bring him back.

That night and the following nights, I asked Zeena to sleep with me on the big bed. When the memories became too overwhelming, we would sleep downstairs on the sofa, or share the small bed in her room. For weeks after I came home, I vegetated. Maybe it was the jet lag. Maybe it was the overwhelming reality of our home, where every room, every object, was a reminder of Rau. I just sat and stared. I couldn't concentrate on the book I was reading, or on any task I began. I was overwhelmed by all the chores and the business I had to attend to, and so I did nothing. I did not even fix my hair or my face. What for? I had no reason to be beautiful. I took long naps at odd hours of the day, only to wake up in the middle of the night and stay awake like a zombie. Memories of Rau and his presence took over the minutes and hours of my time. Scenes of him flitted in and out at odd hours of the day and night, playing themselves over and over in my mind like an old movie. I would find myself crying over a silly object or a song playing on the radio, and I would cry until my eyes were red and puffy and my head throbbed painfully because my tears would not stop.

I wanted to visit his grave at all moments of the day and night. I longed to talk to him. I would find myself with flowers and candles in hand, driving to the memorial park just to be beside him, to tell him how much I missed him. One night I dreamed of him. I was pregnant and he was embracing me, caressing my tummy and softly saying, "C'mon, love, you can do it. Go ahead, you can do it." He then smiled as he looked at my worried face. I wondered about the meaning of the dream. Why was I pregnant? And how could I be pregnant? In the dream I just knew that I felt so bloated and heavy I could hardly carry myself. That was exactly how I had been feeling the past days. Maybe Rau was reassuring me that he was still with me and was prodding me to go ahead, move on, do what I had to do. He was with me! How could I forget that? We had often talked about being with each other in spirit, beyond time and place, when either of us would go on a trip. Well, he had gone on a one-way trip and he would not be with me physically, but his spirit was with me. How stupid of me to have forgotten our promise to each other!

That dream woke me up. I stopped vegetating. I decided I would remodel our townhouse, just as Rau had planned before he became ill. We wanted to open up the walls of the living and dining rooms so we would have more space and I could see the trees and the sky. We also wanted to have more windows in our bedroom so we could see the sunset and the moonrise. The very next day I hired a contractor and told him how Rau and I had wanted our home to be. Zeena explained how she wanted the terrace to be so she could entertain her friends. In no time the whole house was reverberating with the sounds of five carpenters and masons, hammering, pounding, sawing, and nailing. Dust from the cement walls being torn down covered everything with a thick grey film. Everything was in disarray. Mosquitoes and flies flitted in and out of our bedroom because the screens had been removed. We took our meals at a makeshift table in Zeena's room, which was the only area that was not being remodeled. In a little more than two months, everything was done.

Our home now looked airy and spacious. Everywhere I looked, with no more walls to obstruct the view, I could see the trees and the sky. At night, I could lie on the sofa and see the moon through the fiberglass roof that covered the terrace. And my bedroom became a great place from which to watch a glowing sunset. As a finishing touch, I had the whole house repainted. For the first time since Rau's death, I felt happy and pleased. This was how he had dreamed our home would look. He had been so excited about remodeling it; he said he would take care of everything. He would have been so happy about the sofa in the terrace where he could read his book as the trees swayed above his head. Zeena and I bought a beanbag and a rug for her area. I would find myself sitting on the sofa where he would have been reading a book, but my smile would fade as I felt the tears well in my eyes on realizing that he would never enjoy this new home with me and Zeena. Being together in spirit was not good enough for me. I needed his physical presence, his hugs, his smiling face, his voice, his thoughts, his advice.

Now I was ready to face the more unpleasant tasks that needed to be done. I had to fix his papers as people had advised me to do: his death certificate, his SSS pension, taxes, bank accounts, and insurance. I had postponed doing all these because I knew nothing about them and they would only be more painful reminders that Rau was gone. Now I had to do everything by myself.

The whole process was tedious and boring. Forms had to be filled up, signed, countersigned. I had to line up several times, have the paper signed again, wait, come back. The documents were scrutinized, notarized, publicized, and I was asked to submit supporting papers like Rau's birth certificate, our wedding certificate, his death certificate, employment certificate, hospital bills, medicine bills.

I was a WIDOW. That whole month when I had to go to different offices to declare Rau's death, fix his papers, and settle his accounts, made me realize that. I had to sign the word *widow* innumerable times beside the word *status*. I was a widow at least to the world and the public, even if I personally was not ready to accept the fact. What it meant to me at that time was that I had to do by myself everything Rau used to do. How could he do this to me? He knew I had extreme difficulty keeping track of my checkbook and balancing or juggling my grocery budget. How could he expect me to remember to pay income tax, real estate tax, fire insurance, car insurance, home amortization, condominium dues, car registration, medical insurance? He didn't even tell me where the papers were and he didn't teach me how to go about paying. I vaguely remembered that he had an accountant friend who helped with the computation of our taxes and an efficient secretary who reminded him when payments were due and did the paying herself. I had to consult them.

All this was distressing to me. Being an art teacher, I was used to having things under control: my schedule, my lessons, my students, my art materials, my activities. Suddenly, with Rau's death, I was confronted with things alien to me and over which I had no control. I felt like a student about to take a crucial test but I didn't prepare for it and I knew I would flunk. There was no escape. I had to learn pretty fast. The Bureau of Internal Revenue taught me a costly

162

lesson: stupid, innocent widows are penalized for malingering and grieving. I had to pay a five-figure sum as penalty for the five-month delay in declaring my widowhood. I couldn't afford to make any more mistakes. Learning from this experience, I hired a good lawyer to handle my affairs.

The last straw for me was having my car suddenly stop in the middle of traffic. In the past, I usually left the car and called up Rau from the nearest telephone, and in no time he would be there, no matter how important his meeting was. He knew I didn't know a thing about the car except to drive it. This time I had no Rau to call. My brother came instead, arranged for tow service, and took me home. I cried, frustrated by my helplessness and Rau's absence.

That week, when I went to the memorial park for my regular visits, I had no prayers, candles, or flowers for Rau. I tearfully scolded him instead. I was angry with him for leaving me in the lurch. Using my most vivid language, I related to him all the frustration and humiliation I had suffered in just a few months without him. How could he expect me to continue living, to take care of Zeena and Vicky, our home and the two cars, when I couldn't even take care of myself? No wonder widows remarry, I told him. We need someone to take care of all those hundred and one things husbands ought to do. I was so angry at being helpless that I arranged to sell the two old cars — Rau's and mine — and in exchange I bought myself a brand-new one. I was no longer going to be scared about driving alone at night and getting stalled in traffic, or worse, getting stalled in an empty street. I didn't need to call Rau anymore.

It was several weeks before his grave was brightened up again with flowers and candles. By then, I had contacted our old friends who were more than happy to help me out and were just waiting for my call. Male friends took me out to dinner and asked how I was coping. They offered to take over the paperwork on documents I couldn't understand. But they were a little cautious in relating to me, as though my being a widow had changed me as a person.

It was a pleasant surprise to receive from Rau's friends in his old radio company a check for life insurance they had given him as a benefit. A long time friend of Rau's, now a vice president at an insurance company, asked if I had received all the insurance benefits due me. I told him I didn't know. I told him about my traumatic experience with the BIR after which I vowed not to follow up any more papers. Being asked questions by officers of different companies and not knowing the answers made me feel dumb, angry, frustrated. Rau's friend prodded me to do a follow-up, for Rau's sake, but I couldn't be persuaded. A lawyer friend of ours could do that for me, I said. Besides, I told him I didn't want to have to write *widow* on any more forms. I didn't feel like a widow. I felt very much married, except that by God's strange plans, my partner had gone ahead of me. It wasn't true what the marriage vows said: "Till death do us part." That was a lie. Death only made me more acutely aware of Rau's presence now than when he was alive. His friend gave me a sympathetic smile, and I knew he was thinking I was crazy and probably just overcome by grief. I kept quiet and thanked him for his help.

Driving home from his office, I thought about Rau and how much I missed him. I forgave him all his faults and shed tears of regret at all the angry words I had thrown at him during our quarrels. I blamed myself for not having been more caring, more attentive, more solicitous when he was sick. I regretted all the times I had gone abroad, precious days I should have spent with him, had I known he would go so soon. I recalled all our little arguments and big fights and I cried for having hurt him.

After that day, I didn't want to go out again. I didn't want to see couples walking together, holding hands the way Rau and I had done. Whenever I saw two people in a restaurant or just walking with their arms around each other, tears would well in my eyes immediately, and I would long for Rau's presence, his arms around me, his hands holding mine. I would choke with the pain of my longing and often I had to stop the car because I couldn't see through my tears. It was a miracle I didn't get into any car accident that first year.

The impact of Rau's absence became even more intense a little more than a year later. It was Zeena's first year of college. She chose to go to the University of the Philippines Manila, even though we were just five minutes away from the Diliman campus. It was her way of declaring her growth and independence. The blow came when she excitedly told me, "Mom, I'm going to live in the dorm near UP Manila, with my sorority friends, so you don't have to take me to school and I won't be too tired travelling through the traffic." I was emotionally torn. On the one hand, I was happy that she was asserting her independence and was ready to live on her own. On the other hand, I was afraid, afraid to lose her and miss her, her noise and clutter, her affectionate presence, her countless friends all over the house, filling the terrace with their laughter and talk and singing. I was afraid to be alone. I wanted to hold her back, beg her to stay, because I hadn't even gotten used to Rau's absence and now I was going to lose her too.

Her excitement about moving immediately to her own dorm pained me. I knew the pull of her new friends, her new school, and new college experiences was stronger than her need to be with me. In her youthful excitement, she did not see the fear and pain in my eyes as I said good-bye to her. Her leaving, so soon after Rau died, plunged me into a new depression that intensified my feeling of abandonment. Psychologists call this period when all the children are gone from home the "empty nest syndrome." But I had only one child. There were no other children to cushion the blow of Zeena's leaving and there was no husband to share the empty nest with. As a result, I suffered from the "empty heart and home" syndrome with Rau also gone. That year I suffered not only because I was missing a husband, but also because I lost a child.

I had not been ready for Rau's death; I was not ready for Zeena's leaving only one year later. The emptiness echoed throughout the house, in each of the rooms and in every corner of my heart. I dreaded coming home, for there were no sounds of laughter or the heavy footsteps of teenagers or noisy rock music. My one consolation at home was Vicky, who distracted me with her chatter and her cooking. Once again what sustained me during that depressing time was my gang of women friends in the subdivision, my best friends,

165

and our spiritual group. We celebrated birthdays throughout the year with noisy, happy dinners, shopping sprees, and gift-giving. On events like Valentine's Day, my birthday, and holidays, my best friends were there. They stayed with me, allowing me to cry and express my pain while making sure I didn't drown in my misery. In a lighter vein, they hinted about matching me with their single brothers, or with their friends who were either separated or widowed. I could only laugh at all their valiant attempts because a romantic new relationship was farthest from my mind. Rau's presence in my life was still too strong for me to even consider having another man.

Besides, I assured my women friends, I was blessed with true and lasting friendships with a few men I had known since high school. They had remained my friends even after I got married, and Rau eventually became their friend as well. The others were friends Rau and I had met after we married, and with them we shared many experiences—political, emotional, and spiritual—having been fellow protesters during the martial-law years. They now provided the male companionship I needed, the shoulders to cry on when the pain of missing Rau overwhelmed me. I called them up whenever I had problems with Rau's papers or my car or when bringing up Zeena as a single parent became difficult. And they respected my wish to stop matching me with every available bachelor or separated man, for I told them I had many great years with Rau and that was enough.

ON MY THIRD YEAR of widowhood, I was bothered by my utter lack of physical and sexual attraction to other men. That was strange to me because even when Rau was still alive, I would react like a woman when I saw an attractive man.

Now there was nothing. I felt sexless. Was I nearing menopause? Was I undergoing a midlife crisis? Was there something wrong with me? Why wasn't I reacting to the overtures of men around me? Why was I deliberately trying to look shoddy and dowdy? Why had I lost all the excitement I used to find in shopping, dressing up, changing my hairstyle? I didn't react to men as men when they were around.

My psychologist-friend quieted my fears and worries. She told me that what I was going through was normal: I was still grieving. It takes time, she assured me, just follow your feelings and allow yourself to grieve. My other women friends also assured me that I was still an attractive woman even if I didn't feel like one. Their constant reassurance about the ordinariness of my new state of "unwomanness" made me accept my grief as normal for widows like myself.

But their being married and having a husband while I was a widow and alone made me feel suddenly alienated from them. I felt incomplete without Rau. For a time, I felt awkward attending couples parties alone. And even if there were singles in our group, they were comfortable being so, while I winced every time I saw my friends who were couples. I used to be part of a couple! Now I was alone and feeling strange about it.

My friends had their husbands, I thought, so how can they feel what I'm going through? How could they know the depths of my loneliness? How could I explain that I was lonely but at the same time I did not want another man? I wanted Rau. I was lonely for him. And every time I saw men in our group, I remembered that Rau had been a part of them. The memory was too painful. For a time, I withdrew from our couples group and sought out widows like myself. I was surprised to find that there were many of us — at all stages of life. We formed a group and started going out together, especially on romantic days like Valentine's. We had group dinners and picnics at the beach. We were having so much fun that the single girls and career women soon joined our other activities, sharing and praying sessions, birthday and anniversary celebrations. But the lonely moments would still come now and then, in spite of the companionship of other widows. It did help to realize that each of us had our lonely moments to cope with, and that we could share the experience with each other even if we had to go through it alone.

School work and activities with friends Rau and I treasured somehow stabilized my life and made Zeena's absence less conspicuous. I looked forward to the weekend, when I would fetch Zeena from her dorm and we would go out for a late breakfast or lunch, and then drive over to the malls for leisurely shopping or a movie. I would be very disappointed when she called home to say she had a party that weekend and wouldn't be coming home. Dinner would then be a solitary affair with Vicky consoling me or putting me to sleep while we reminisced about Rau. The year Zeena went off to live in the dorm, I changed my matrimonial bed into a single bed. After all, I was now truly single, alone in the house.

After a year, Zeena, now a junior, gave up dorm life. We were also able to get a condominium in Mandaluyong closer to both her school and mine, so we could avoid Quezon City's horrendous traffic. The new place became our Monday to Friday dorm, for we still went home on weekends to our townhouse from which it was easier to visit Rau and have Sunday dinner with my sister and her family. It was the convenient location that Zeena liked most about the condo because now her special friend could take her home every day. His visits had been limited to weekends because it took him two hours just to visit her from his home in Manila. In other words, it was primarily for love that Zeena gave up her dorm, and that was good enough reason for me to rejoice. Besides, having her boyfriend around was like having another member of the family. Zeena's newfound relationship excited me because it allowed me to relive my own times with Rau. While she shared with me the ups and downs of her romance, I shared with her my memories of my first boyfriend, my other special friends, and finally, how I met her father and how we fell in love. Slowly, our weekends together became dependent on her weekend plans with her friend. More and more I saw that Zeena's life was shared with her classmates and special friend and less with me. She was not my little girl anymore; she was blooming into a young lady, quite independent and mature.

Zeena and I had new conflicts and quarrels the fourth year after Rau died. I felt she was too independent, assertive, irresponsible. I was having difficulty playing both father and mother to her. I had never been good at being strict, but now I had to be, for Rau was no longer around to deal with Zeena. Our tearful confrontations left me feeling like a failure. Why was Rau not around when I needed him most?

Several heart-to-heart talks with my women friends gave me a new perspective on solo parenting. They told me I had to accept my limitations and learn to be more relaxed with Zeena. Finally, after several emotional encounters with her, I realized I was at fault—I was trying too hard to make up for Rau's absence by being him and me both with our daughter. But it wasn't working. I was frustrated and Zeena was rebellious. Feeling emotionally exhausted, I talked to her, told her how much of a failure I felt myself to be, and apologized for being so hard on her, while explaining that I was simply making up for her father's absence. We ended up in each other's arms, crying and apologizing for our unreasonable behavior towards each other.

Zeena showed me the way and told me how to cope. "Mom, Dad is gone. Don't try too hard to be mom and dad to me. Just be a mom. You're still young. Go out, have dates. Get married again!" I looked with surprise at my daughter, finally realizing that she was not a child but a mature young adult, a truly wise person. All this time I had been treating her like a little girl, not realizing she had grown up and was wiser and more adult than I gave her credit for. She was her own person. And now she was advising me to let go and teaching me how.

Her words made me realize I had to make a shift. It was time. It had been four years since Rau died and I had to make my own life. What Zeena said was true: Rau was physically gone in spite of my vivid awareness of his presence. I was a single parent, a single person. She didn't need as much supervision anymore. I could—and should—live my own life, do what I wanted to do.

I started to follow her advice. I stopped breathing down her neck and allowed her more freedom and independence. I plunged into new involvements in the professional and women's groups I belonged to. I initiated projects that had long-term goals and would benefit more people. It was my way of returning in kind all the talents and blessings God had given me. Now, while I was still strong and healthy, I wanted to use them in projects that would help others.

Slowly, too, I was getting used to being alone and not being lonely being alone. It was a strange feeling being "single" again. I began to enjoy my new "single-ness," accepting that Rau had gone ahead of me, leaving me alone. It was like getting to know myself all over again, only this time it was an older, more mature me. With this new feeling, I found no urgent need to have someone to take Rau's place just yet, as Zeena had advised. Besides, aside from my women friends I had my male friends to talk to and go out with when I wanted to. I liked it that way, relishing the special friendship I had with each of them. With Rau gone, I could now share the feelings I had previously shared only with him and my women friends. The result was a new and deeper relationship with my male friends that I hadn't had with them when I was married, and it was beautiful because we made no demands on each other, only caring and concern and the readiness to be available when I needed them or when they needed me. They gave me the space I wanted because I needed time to be acquainted with myself again, not as wife or mother to someone, but as myself, a single person. I had to ask new questions of myself because all this time my future had been planned together with Rau.

Now there was no Rau in my life, and soon Zeena would be leaving to make her own life. I would be alone. What did I want my life to be this coming year? These coming two, four, seven, ten years? Suddenly, the prospect of the future excited me. I have long wanted to have a children's museum where all kinds of children could draw and paint and carve, sing and dance and act, so that they could discover what great and beautiful creatures they are. I want to continue giving art workshops to teachers in the provinces and to people who think they are not good in art. I want to paint the whole day, and do crafts and work with my hands. I want to live beside the beach and sleep with the sound of the waves. I want to go to undiscovered places in the Philippines and to faraway places in the world like Kathmandu ... read poetry and write ... play the flute ... learn a sport I'm not good at. I want enough time to enjoy Zeena and my family and my friends in a place without traffic and pollution. I want to work not for a living but because I want to share all the experiences, the talents, the blessings I have. And I want time not working, not doing, but just being....

It was exhilarating to plan and to be excited about the future, but I knew I had not completely let go of Rau. My attachment to him and to Zeena was revealed in a vivid dream I had which I recalled only because I was asked to remember it in a dream workshop facilitated by a friend who was a dream analyst and counselor. In that dream I was in a big house with plenty of people. There was a party. I was by myself in a room, wearing only shorts and slippers. Suddenly, Rau came in, natty in a dark blue suit. I asked him if he was dressed because of the party. He said no, he was going somewhere. I want to go with you, I said, wait for me because I have to dress up. I hurriedly got my clothes and was dressing up when I heard Rau's footsteps. He was going downstairs. I rushed to the window. Down below in the driveway, I saw him and Zeena, who was also dressed, enter a car. Hey, wait for me! I shouted. Wait for me! They did not seem to hear me and they drove away. I cried in frustration and anger. It was so unlike Rau to just go and leave me. I woke up from my dream in tears.

In the workshop, I was crying again as I recounted the dream. The facilitator asked me what it meant to me. I told him that it was true, Rau had gone ahead of me and he didn't say good-bye. And Zeena was soon leaving me too. But my insight as to the reason I was feeling frustrated and angry was that after all these four years I hadn't really let go of them both and I wasn't ready to let them go because things had happened too fast and too soon. I hardly had time for a proper good-bye. The facilitator then asked me to dream the dream again and create the ending I wanted it to have. For a few minutes, I closed my eyes and played back the dream in my mind. At the point where Rau came into the room dressed in a dark blue suit, I stopped him and held his hand. I told him, "Rau, I know you are going to leave me, but before you go, please say good-bye to me. Embrace me tightly. Give me a big kiss and a warm hug. Say 'I love you' to me as you usually do." And he did as I asked him. Then Zeena came into the room, all dressed too, and I told her exactly the same things

I had told Rau. I hugged both of them tightly for a long time. When it was time for them to go, I said, "I want to be the one to say good-bye. So please go slowly." They walked to the car, but before they got in, they turned to me and waved their hands in farewell, and I said in a loud voice, "Good-bye, Rau ... good-bye, Zeena...." I waved my hand until the car was some distance away and I couldn't see their faces anymore.

After relating this revised ending of my dream to the group, I was still in tears but I felt greatly relieved. It was good to be the one to say good-bye. It took me four long years to realize I hadn't really let go of Rau and Zeena, and my dream told me I had to. It was only after the dream that I could think of facing the future alone. Zeena was right. Rau has gone ahead of me, but I'm still young and I feel strong. There is a future ahead of me.

It has been four long years since Rau's death and I have only just begun to say good-bye. I have only just begun to realize what the word *widow* means. I guess it means realizing that the pain of loss and missing, like a big, gaping wound deep in the soul, will never disappear. The difference is that after four years it is easier to accept the reality, like getting adjusted to having only one breast while the other is one big, blank, flat wound on my chest, making me feel incomplete physically. Losing Rau was like losing half of me. I was incomplete without him. And at this point I do not know if I'll ever feel complete again. I guess I have to allow others to come into my life by shelving all my memories of Rau and stacking them neatly like pictures in a photo album, to be recalled at will. I must sweep aside mementos and recollections of Rau that I luxuriously scatter in the rooms of my mind, ready to be picked up and rolled around and enjoyed over and over again when a familiar tune or an object like a rose brings it into focus, and the beauty of his unconditional love for me brings fresh tears to my eyes.

How do I fold neatly eighteen years of being loved and loving this man who was so tender and kind and generous and wise, who loved music and reading and quiet moments, who taught me to be still so I could watch the sunset and the moonrise, who was also at times so unreasonable and possessive and hardheaded I could cry in sheer frustration, but who loved me so completely I was secure and complacent, taking for granted that we would live "happily ever after"? I guess being a widow, I can never neatly tuck away so many years of memories. Somehow, in unguarded moments, a recollection here or a memory there slips out and the tears come pouring and the old feelings rush in as fresh as on the day it happened.

I have moved on these past four years from being an angry, perplexed, and tearful widow, to being a relatively contented, wiser, and smiling widow. I look back and feel blessed for the richness and loving of the years I shared with Rau: for eighteen years, on the sixteenth of every month (to commemorate June 16th, the day we were married), I was reminded that he thought himself very lucky for marrying me and he had to celebrate by giving me a gift: flowers, a book, or a romantic dinner for two. How can I not feel rich with the two hundred sixteen wedding anniversaries we celebrated? I'm sure no other couple has celebrated as many.

Now I look forward and see myself so full and ready to share, not only with one person but with many others, all that loving Rau gave me. I feel for others all the pain and anger and frustration, because Rau and I went through many rough times too. Being a widow, I feel that my love is no longer singular but plural, shared with so many more people, and I feel loved in return by men and women who care for me deeply.

Will I ever look for another person to take Rau's place? Will I ever love another man the way I loved him? Will someone love me in the same way or will love be different the next time? Will I find someone who can make me set Rau aside and start a new life all over again and believe in "happily ever after"? Will I be ready to commit my life to one man again, to share a future? Right now I don't feel the urgency to look for "a man" or to consider the several candidates my friends offer me. I am enjoying my new "single blessedhood" and getting used to being more friend than mother to Zeena. We have only a few years together before she starts her own family and I want to enjoy those years. Maybe, when she is gone and married and I'm all alone, this need for another man will become more urgent. Maybe, when I meet a man with Rau's intensity and unconditional loving and need of me, Rau's presence will become a pleasant memory.

Until that time, I shall be fascinated by my present state. I'm slowly exploring and savoring all the nuances of being a widow, enjoying the friendship and sisterhood of my daughter, my only sister, Rau's sisters and mother, my women friends, my fellow widows, and my single friends. Their sensitivity to my aloneness and loneliness has led me to enjoy new levels of caring and supportive awareness which I would not have known were I still blissfully married.

And my friendships with my male friends have opened up to me a new vocabulary of loving beyond sex and physical intimacy. It is tender soul-caring that nourishes and affirms my being a woman without asking, in exchange, for anything I am not ready to give just yet. They respected my need for physical distance while I was grieving my loss, and yet they gave me the emotional closeness and masculine companionship I needed during the many moments I missed Rau.

With the richness and loving given to me by my friends, male and female, I am now ready to face being a widow. They have healed the pain of my loss by their constant presence; they have helped me scale the emotional heights and depths of my widowhood by their unconditional caring, loving, and affirming of my femaleness. Now, with a new sense of adventure and risk, I feel like an adolescent again, a little awkward but excited at being a single woman the second time around.

FREEDOM TO BE

MA. AGNES O. PRIETO

"Oh dear
what can I do
Baby's in black
and I'm feeling blue
Yes ... oh what can I do?"

DEAR Ms. Manners ... and Dr. Holmes, Tiya Dely, and Tito Vannie,

Help! I'm at my wits' end! You've tackled every awkward social situation and aberration, but you've left us out totally, we free spirits in midlife. Sure, we're a slightly more complex social issue than choking on chicken bones at a sit-down dinner. For one, it's impossible to categorize us. Ms., Miss, Mrs. or Mistress? As a free spirit, I must tell you right now that my one main achievement in life has been to defy classification.

When I was younger, I allowed society to box me in, but I realized how limiting that all was. There is nothing more sexist than monosyllabic titles. They all hinge one's relationship on a "Mr." A Miss is usually what the word implies: someone society perceives as having missed out on something just because she doesn't have a man.

Poor things, it's all they can do to justify their existence without the opposite sex, just because they have opted to go it all alone. Two misses I know are most harassed creatures at parties, pressured as they are by mesdames who egg them on to marriage or some form of relating even as their own marriages are on the rocks. What the majority don't realize is, there is life without a man and it can be a great one too, once a girl does away with otherwise silly ideas about men and how indispensable they are to her happiness.

To be a Mrs. is what they teach us to aspire for. As soon as a girl can say "boy," she is brought up thinking that all of life builds up for the one main event — marriage. It definitely is a social highlight. I married my first husband because I was tired of parties and I had been to all the discos every other night. My friends were dying to have an event to really dress up for, and so I had a morning wedding by the beach to which guests came as Victorian beauties because they were so sure all the girls would be dressed up as Hawaiian wahines and they wanted to stand out. But after the thank-you notes had been sent out, I found myself at a dead end. One has to be very inventive if one is to survive as a Mrs. At some point, one gets brainwashed into believing that the discovery of a new barbecue marinade is as momentous an event as Einstein's discovery of the theory of relativity. I should know. Such was my faith in what people thought was best for me that I actually became a Mrs. twice. Carrying someone's name boxed me into roles that I enjoyed playing, up to a point.

Then I wanted out.

Nowadays I am Ms. and carrying my very own name. I decided to go back to this most precious legacy from my parents when I got an ultimatum from friends who were tired of shifting my name(s) around in their address books under different letters of the alphabet. They told me, rather tersely, that there was only one more slot left for me and I could no longer change names (or status). I opted to be just me, status undetermined.

Ms. Manners, I used to not care whether I was in good form or not as long as I was comfortable with myself. And Dr. Holmes, I and my

Subconscious were enjoying this rather pleasurable relationship so there was no need to consult you or Tiya Dely or Tito Vannie. I was so certain I would go on forever. Now, suddenly, the signs are on the wall ....

These days I seem to spend more time at the beauty parlor, but with less favorable results. I used to think it was the new hairdresser. Now I know better. The traitorous grey peeps through my locks anyway despite new hands and with just one washing my hair winds up tricolored — carrot, brown, and black. It's happened overnight, and it isn't the hairdresser's fault.

The same phenomenon extends to my work at the gym. I used to go merely for the dancing, but now I have to work and work hard on my abs, my outer thighs, my shoulders, my chest. Again, the results have been minimal. No matter what I do, the middle spread manages to catch up, with cruel tenacity, with the rest of me.

All of a sudden, glasses have become my most valuable possession. Without them, the printed word is one big blur; menus, reports, credit card invoices, and books are suddenly inaccessible. And my memory — where have I left it? I had it with me only a while ago, but now I can't recall where I might have placed it. Would someone, anyone who finds it kindly send it back please to .... uh ... I can't remember my address.

Most alarming, though, is the devastation my psyche is going through. For three years, it seems, I have been on the verge of a breakdown. It's as if the very foundations I have built my life on are going through a terrible shakedown and I can't explain why. What's worse is the overwhelming grief that engulfs me. I grieve, for what, I do not know. Most times I want to hide away, to crawl under the covers and wait for this terrible time to pass.

But it simply won't go away. Unlike the spooks of my childhood that faded away in the light of morning, this is unrelenting. The nameless grief intensifies, the middle age spread becomes more conspicuous, and the carrot-colored strands turn flaming orange against the dull grey. Outwardly, I maintain my cool, try to anyway, but who is this crone shrieking at the cook for having burned the toast? It's me. Where is the nubile young thing who ran around town in hot pants? She was just around here a couple of days ago. Now she's gone forever, transformed into this matron panting hotly up the steps.

Still, the Big Denial goes on. This is a rewrite, something I have never, ever, in my entire writing career had to do. Those futile attempts to fit into a micromini, the bouts with the dermatologist, the torture sessions with the dentist. (They're all part of the Big Coverup which deceives no one except myself. And the list goes on and on.) All my life I have been able to get away with practically anything, except murder, which I have contemplated once or twice but never had the guts to carry out. Getting Away With It was the operative theme that ran through my life. I came to this realization early on in my adulthood and built a pretty exciting life around it. I loved it. Not for me were rules and regulations that governed lesser mortals. Icarus-like, I flew into the face of the sun countless times and never had a wing singed. With the confidence of a freed spirit, I "slipped the surly bonds of earth and danced the sky on laughter silvered wings."

I had earned my freedom. Early on in life, I had been freed by my confrontation with pain and searing sorrow, death and desolation. (Would you want me to guest on your program, Tiya Dely? Or maybe I shall write a script for Mother Lily based on my soap opera of a life and earn big bucks.) I was only in my twenties, barely into adulthood, and pregnant with my third child when my first husband died. In one fell swoop I had to grapple with death and life. Suddenly, I was thrust from the cushion of young suburban matronhood into a struggle for survival. I learned to understand my grief, to befriend it, and I turned my crisis around. Before I could live again, I had to understand death and separation, and my only armor was my vulnerability.

Vulnerability opened wonderfully fascinating doors for me. A wise old Jesuit whispered the secret to me: your strength, he said, is your vulnerability. The fact that I was unarmed by rules and ordinances in turn disarmed. Now a deep-sea diver, Icarus took the plunge and was rewarded with sights not for the faint-hearted. The depths of the ocean were dark and cold initially but farther on they revealed glorious treasures bequeathed by sunken ships and exotic flora and fish that had never seen the light of day. The implication of death and separation was transitoriness. Everything was in a state of passage, like fish floating by. Even deep down under the sea nothing ever remained the same. What was essential was the NOW. The plunge. The breathtaking beauty of the undersea. I did away with the past and never thought about the future. It was the present I lived for. I tried to learn not to have attachments, to anyone or anything, knowing that anyway they would die or, like fish, swim away. I had experiences instead — brief, supercharged relatings that always took my breath, and my heart, away. It was then I discovered that whether I was Ms. or Miss or Mrs., none of it was a guarantee against heartbreak.

Each plunge was unplanned, spontaneous, free. Always there was the moment of choice when, poised to take the dive, I saw my options flash before my eyes. There was the implication of flight but it was only a free fall, for the exhilaration of letting go hastened the descent. Then there was the impact on the ground. Eventually, I learned to take the tumble too. Even the hardness of the ground became familiar, almost a friend. It was part of being free, or so I thought. In retrospect, I was more of a freed spirit in flight, not in upward soaring but in escape. Instead of relationships, I had experiences. When they threatened to blossom into full commitment, I took flight, which I mistook for freedom.

A well-loved mentor has told me that by now, a remarriage and many relationships hence, she thinks I might have acquired a handle on life and its heartbreak, if not on loving. But here I am again, beset by fresh grieving. It's all I can do to yoga and tai-chi and meditate it all away. Life as a free spirit, as you can see, has not been all soaring; it has not been without pain.

At the silver jubilee of my high school class, my classmates, girls I had grown up with, told me they could not figure out why someone as "blessed" and fortunate as I would choose the route I had taken.

They looked askance when I proudly displayed the medals of merit I have awarded myself for surviving and getting out of my second marriage. And they threatened to have me put in a straitjacket (were it not for our many years of shared childhood memories) for signing away my shares of stock, my vice-chairpersonship, my antiques, my house, etcetera, as I ended that marriage. They think I have gone absolutely bonkers. But this, to me, is what it means to be free — to be able to walk away without baggage, material or psychological, to go on with my search, unimpeded by excess luggage. I travel very light, carrying only my commitment to the truth of my self.

It is not an easy search. That's why there are so few free spirits about. Oh sure, everyone is tickled pink when he/she is described as free. Manila society's so-called Dynasty Girls feel they have a franchise on it, but as one of them would say, there are very few truly freed spirits in Manila. Most of them think being a free spirit is having the ability to do whatever one wants. One throws in economic freedom as part and parcel of it all. Another emphasizes the responsibility that goes along with the freedom. I guess these are all characteristics that describe the state, but there's got to be something more to breaking rules and getting away with it (and looking glamorous in the process). There must be a larger framework that allows for transcendence into a totally new paradigm of acting and feeling and thinking in which one is fully attuned to one's highest, truest nature. It does not mean breaking rules all the time. It's more about being true to one's self. One can be a quiet little housewife in the surburbs and still be a free spirit.

This is why pain is integral to freedom. To be free means not to brook hypocrisy and untruth, and most times this is difficult to achieve. But, like I say, I am a veteran of pain, Tiya Dely, and I could give your most popular heroine a run for her money. I thought death was familiar, for I have seen it too many times in my life. But my mother died more than a year ago and it still wracks me with pain just to think about her passing. This time the pain goes deep down beneath the old scars, a ruthless surgical knife that exhumes buried feelings. In many ways, I have not come to a full acceptance that my

180

mother will never again be and I will never have the chance to show her how much I love her. Initially, I thought it was the depth of my regret that caused me to mourn. I know that it goes even deeper. Unconsciously, my mother stood for life, and with her passing I am forced to come face to face with my own mortality. Now I realize I am mourning the passing of my own life from young adulthood towards maturity. As I enter a phase of life which signals finality, it is my own death I grieve.

There are no rites of passage to mark this point in a woman's life, no rituals to signify the critical changes happening within and to invoke the gods' blessings for the new stage that lies ahead. I only know that all of a sudden I feel blue and the crying spells just can't seem to stop.

Ms. Manners, you must come up with a new set of good manners and right conduct that will enable the rest of the world to deal with the much dreaded menopause. For unlike the other periods in a woman's life — her birth, puberty, marriage, and childbirth — no one in polite society will refer to this one. It is a much misunderstood phase that many choose to see as the end. Our youth-oriented culture perceives it as a fate worse than death. But what is it really? Biologically, there is an ovarian transition that results in the final cessation of menstruation. Of course, it's so much more complex than all that, a five- to seven-year phase when women gradually stop ovulating, with all the attendant hormonal changes that now translate into the aging process which subconsciously I mourn.

We have no guidelines, perhaps because in the past most women did not live long enough to go beyond menopause. My one other experience of this state is that of my mother, and she handled this season as she did most things in life — with grace and humor. We all knew what she was going through but we never felt the inconvenience of seeing her suffer. She in fact had lots of fun after she learned to deal with the hot flashes and sweating. Unconsciously, she must have been going through some rite of passage. She transformed herself from a mother who was dead serious about her duties (she would not even allow me to "pollute" my mind with "cheap" romantic novels) into a friend who was carefree and understanding. As she freed herself, one of the first things she did was to buy for herself an entire set of the romantic novels she had once rallied against. She gathered her friends together and they would go "banjing," a word they concocted for "bumming around." That wasn't like my mother at all. She had always been a purposeful woman to whom bumming around seemed sacrilegious. But bum around she did. In the afternoons, she would pick up her friends and they would go out for merienda and talk. We were all at boarding school then and she was quite alone at home. Eventually, she would learn to play mah-jongg. She did not know about HRT, hormone replacement therapy, which fills in the estrogen and the progestin once produced by the body that would have allowed her to resume her normal, youthful female functions. Instead, she turned to playing with the "ivory keys," as she called the therapy that would work well for her the rest of her life. Everyone in the family learned to live with this little "mania" of hers.

How would it have been, Ms. Manners, if there had been a ceremony to mark my mother's passage into that new stage of her life? Would she have been happier had she passed through the three stages described by Mankowitz? First, the stage of isolation, the withdrawal from society and into close contact with nature. This would have made my mother's passage easier, for it would have allowed her to go inside herself and contemplate the changes within her without fear of being misunderstood. The second stage is a ritual, symbolic of the severance. The actual onset of menopause might have eased the pain of confrontation with death. The third phase, a ceremony of rebirth and renewal, would have announced the return to society of a new, changed woman, no longer just mother or wife, but a being all her own.

And what if she had known about HRT, the hottest thing in the West these days? Research has proven that it prevents osteoporosis or the loss of bone mass, decreases the possibility of heart attack, and does away with hot flashes. HRT has also been known to reduce insomnia, which causes great misery to women of this age; it also greatly improves energy, not only allowing a woman to maintain a productive life but enhancing it so that she experiences a new sense of well-being. Everyone on HRT attests to renewed sexual interest and comfort, to the delight of their partners and to their own great satisfaction. Many of the negative connotations attached to menopause have come from men who see the cessation of sex as life-threatening. HRT has also been proven to improve concentration and memory and it may increase longevity. In a nutshell, HRT may just be the fountain of youth women have been looking for.

But doctors also warn against the possibility of increased risk of cancer of the uterus and breast swelling or pain due to HRT. Ironically, it also may cause menstruation and all its syndromes to continue.

The rites of passage, HRT — these would have provided my mother the societal and physical/emotional framework within which to work out her dramatic life shift. And, as a takeoff point for this final stage, to delve into the soul which transcends it all. It is now possible to flex the soul muscles, to strengthen them through the transformation technologies available to any and every type of soul seeking. In times past, this kind of knowledge was hidden, accessible only to hermits in their mountain lairs. Today, it can be had at any bookstand. And there are any number of support groups to help bring on the "technology transfer" through transcendental meditation, hatha or physical yoga, tai-chi or dynamic meditation. One can allot 20 minutes a day to a practice or one can choose an entirely new life-style dedicated to greater wholistic health. It's entirely up to one's need to transform the difficulties of change and the challenge to grow even further. Transformation technologies offer new paradigms, entirely fresh frameworks within which to live out life with the fullest of joy.

All these three thrusts could help flesh out what Gail Sheehy, the author of *Silent Passage*, says: that the midlife passage is the beginning of a long and little mapped stage of postreproductive life, what she terms the Second Adulthood. It also has three stages: perimenopause, or the start of the transition; menopause, or the completion of ovarian transition; and a stage Sheehy calls coalescence, defined as "the mirror image of adolescence," a time for sourcing into a new zest, a renewed lifespring which comes about from integration, a coming to terms with the many fragmentations that beset a woman when she is younger. It is a potent time of great inner wealth, a period of dramatic shift in the psychological, physical, social, and spiritual aspects of a woman's life rather than the bleak and barren wasteland it has been portrayed to be.

Right now I'm undergoing the perimenopause panic. It is not quite menopause yet. My libido is still intact; my organs are functioning. No hot flashes overwhelm me. But the intimations of mortality are loud and clear. Pretty soon my estrogen levels will go down to nil; my reproductive capacities will have gone to seed. The grey strands are not only embarrassing, they are an affront to my being, the one I invented and reinvented to fit into the patterns of youthfulness that seem to be the only acceptable way to live. I have avoided matronhood like the plague. I dress young — I like hairbands and walking shorts. I go on dates and avoid sit-down dinners. I keep my consciousness fresh, trying never to weigh down my feelings and thoughts with negative baggage. I live young, no mah-jongg sessions please. Anything that smacks of aging is taboo. Give me only cause-oriented projects, consciousness-raising activities, and fun times with my children, who are now 19, 16, 14 ... and two. With the first three, I alternate between being a with-it older groupie and an outrageously eccentric mom. I know I have aged because when I go to their school I no longer get mistaken for a high school senior; people address me as Ma'am. With my two-year-old, I am a young, doting mom again, putting together birthday parties and Halloween costumes. Up to now, I have been able to get away with both roles, enjoying the shock on the faces of young mothers when I tell them I have an adult son too.

I have been blessed with children whose first name is Tolerance. But tolerance has its limits and having me as both father and mother is not easy on anyone.

If there is anything I regret about my life-style, it is the realization that my children are "walking wounded." I am constantly assailed by this question: Would they have been happier if I had lived a more conventional life? This greatly complicates my perimenopause. All the life changes my children and I have been through together are taking their toll now as they stand on the brink of adulthood. I realize that, like me, they have all the potential for strength within them, waiting to be drawn out from a crisis-ridden childhood. I remember the day I told them I had gotten out of a marriage. We were at an Italian place, and incongruously, I was ordering pizza while breaking the news. My second son was in tears. We were out of a family. Overnight, without any warning. We had only the clothes on our backs. For school the following day, we had to rush to a department store to buy more clothes. We never went back to our house again. I left behind my antiques and china and silverware and paintings. At some point, my ex-husband gave me back my jewelry and the children's clothes.

For sometime now I have been caught up in trying to get back on my feet legally, emotionally, financially. I have only a faint idea of the travails the children are going through. My own grief assails me, blinds me to their pain. But we must all walk, wounded as we all are, to wherever it is we have to go.

We shall survive, somehow, that terrible transit. I wait for the phoenix to rise above the ashes. I am still waiting. Meantime, I must deal with the children. My past orientation would have told me to set aside my own pain and allow them theirs so they can also heal and integrating all they have been through, get on to adulthood. I realize now that we can all process these together. The pain has brought us together; we will rise above and beyond it as a unit. Our psyches are finding healing as we find ourselves on parallel paths. They are on their way to First Adulthood. I am on my way to the Second.

First Adulthood is something we are all familiar with. The Second is the gift of modern medical technology to us. It is essentially the realization that midlife means just that—we are only halfway through. Beyond this transition is a new life waiting to be lived. The physical discomforts can now be transcended. We have to deal only with the consciousness. We are the baby boomers, the first of our generation to approach menopause, that dreaded word again. It is not the end; rather, it is a beginning. It is a brand-new playing field, potent with power, where one may create new ways of relating, of giving and receiving. It is definitely more exacting than turning twenty-one.

In First Adulthood, one had to prove one's self, to start from the bottom of the heap. During Second Adulthood, one jumpstarts from the top. The world literally lies at one's feet, done as one is with all the bungling around, the scrounging about, the earnest striving of the first phase. Where one was initially unsure and undecided, here at the mid-point in one's life one is certain about one's strengths and weaknesses. One now possesses the confidence born of painful mistakes. A woman in S.A. is poised, cool, unfazed by it all. But not blasé. Every time is still a tremulous first, fired as she is by this new zest.

I am one with my children in their various life shifts. In my transitions I have come to terms with people's going away. I am still coming to terms, however, with my own going away. The implications of growing old initially push the panic button. But I know that the old solutions — an affair, for instance — will not work anymore. For once, as I approach my Second Adulthood, the dread of my own frailty takes over and I decide that a relationship with a man is not going to cover up the emptiness that gnaws at me. This realization is not the end, though, but a rebirth of a new me who exists beyond the suggestion of masculine thought. This is a Second Adulthood Me, now truly free, particularly from the male projection of what I should be.

All our female lives we are taught to stay within frameworks acceptable to what we were taught was the all-encompassing structure of the male perspective. We were taught to be sweet and compliant and to live up to our gallant's greatest fantasies. Now with hormones going and hair greying, we are suddenly freed from all that. The masculine framework has deemed this phase to be an ending, for the reproductive function is basic to man-woman inter-relating. In the past, this was considered tragic. I now know it to be untrue, and as I contemplate what lies before me, I know I will still exist despite the fact that a man can no longer expect to relate to me as he chooses. Now it is I who chooses how I want to relate to him, and to the world in general. A reborn me is shaking off the shackles of male reference. For once, I am free to just be, for me. "To walk in my own way and be alone; free with an eye to see things as they are," without having to defer decision and process to keep the harmony in relating. I can be as attractive as I choose to be — for my own sake. I can fight for causes all my own now, and lay down my life if I so choose for what I believe in. I can choose to be quiet and live within, or to be part of a moving, dynamic whole.

My body is my own and I go where my spirit leads me.

I look forward to my newfound strength and to independence in all aspects, emotional, spiritual, and financial. Marriage to men of means tied me down considerably in a sense because no matter how hard I worked I could never be equal to their earning capacities. Now I know I don't have to match anyone's income; what is important is to be able to provide the basics and some comforts, as well as to set up something for my future. I know what I can do and not do; I am proud of my skills and I know my limits. Emotionally, my life is no longer focused on the idiosyncrasies of one man. In my spirit life, the one aspect of me that will live on and on (and this I have always worked on), I am in a relationship with the Infinite who is Father-Mother-Child-Lover-All. This is the command position from which I am poised to move on — my period of coalescence, the time of the gathering of strengths. I look forward to getting my act together. Icarus is learning to fly a second time.

Second Adulthood carries with it many privileges not available to those in the First. One of the most precious of these privileges is the freedom to be alone, now that the responsibilities of being care giver are on the wane. Not to relate unless I so choose. Not to take the plunge. To stay, sacrosanct, in my solitude. Being alone holds an allure all its own. Accustomed all my life to juggling a variety of responses — as mother, wife, lover, professional, businessperson, New Age discoverer — I am increasingly enchanted by the thought of total silence in which to create a new me. I have intimations of what delights this may hold when all the children are off to school and I am left to my own devices. The empty nest syndrome that afflicts women left alone after having hinged their entire existence on being mothers, is not for me. However much I love my children and my other relatings to a fault, I look forward to the time when all my duties and responsibilities will have freed me, for new me's. Maybe I'll be an itinerant poet singing and winging my way. Or I could be a sage, tapping into Wisewoman Power and contributing my share of knowledge or creative insight or perhaps, healing, a source of experience and wisdom. This is the ancient role of the Shaman woman which antedates even the medicine man. Or I could become a nun and immure myself behind high walls, shutting the world out to focus on an inner world of relating with the ALL. The possibilities of aloneness are tremendous. I can't wait.

And should there be a lover (the best sex, a conference on older women revealed, is between forty-five and fifty-five), I would want to go beyond the image of myself as mirrored in my lover's eyes, and just be me. It would be a relating free from need and replaced by benevolent giving, not just from lover to beloved but in community with a larger framework of people. He would not define me, nor I him, as is the tendency now. I will no longer need to cater to him nor him to me. Rather, we will enhance and protect each other's being, separate strings in a lyre but singing the same song. And while we will still treasure our togetherness, our freedom will be just as greatly valued: "two solitudes touching each other."

All these will be fueled by a new passion — for an idea, a person, a pursuit; total mental, spiritual, and physical energy which surfaces once one is willing to relinquish the illusion of youth. It's the holding on that saps us, that causes the pain of parting. Initially, I thought you, Ms. Manners, Dr. Holmes, Tiya Dely and Tito Vannie, would help us find the formula that would make it easier to let go, to unleash the power that lies within us, now seemingly obscured by death and extinction. But as we contemplate the passage that stretches out before us, we realize it is only ourselves who will set us free. We have nothing to fear but fear itself.

Sincerely,

Ma. Agnes O. Prieto

SEARCHING FOR ME

TESSIE TOMAS

I N JANUARY 1989, I flew to Los Angeles, California, to try my luck in Hollywood. This was at the prodding of Hal McElroy and Bob Markowitz, the Australian producer and the American director, respectively, of the television movie "A Dangerous Life." At that time I had just broken up with my Norwegian boyfriend, a diplomat assigned in Manila. He had proposed marriage but I candidly told him I was not ready to give up my career in show business to be a diplomat's wife. That declaration hurt him badly and he decided to end our relationship.

I always seem to get caught in an intense relationship just when my career is at its peak. The predicament eventually leads to complications. I would always want to carry on with the relationship but only temporarily, meaning no commitments. Wanting to have my cake and eat it too, I also want to maintain the momentum of my career. Something has to give. Relationships never last.

In March 1989, after staying for two months with an old Filipina friend, I moved to my own apartment along Hollywood Boulevard. I had been auditioning in major Hollywood studios like Paramount, 20th Century Fox, Universal, and Columbia Pictures, as well as the major television stations. I had an agent named Joan Scott whose company, "Writers and Artists," handled stars like Patrick Dreyfuss and Elizabeth McGovern. My schedule was spotty. At times I would have three or four auditions in a week, but at other times I waited in my apartment for a whole month for that precious call from my agent, only to be told that there were no available roles.

Living alone, without my fourteen-year-old son Robin to take care of, away from the pressures of family and friends and a hectic showbiz career, I started to review my life. It was Tessie looking at Tessie from the outside. My mind was like a TV camera zooming away. This had never happened to me before. I had always been caught in a web of unending work and never paused to reflect on where I was. Or to think about what was happening to me and to my personal life. I simply worshipped my career.

After my separation from my husband in 1981, I acquired a new mindset. I would focus all my energies on my career. Nothing and no one would stand in the way of my success. I would love my career. A career is better than a husband. If you take good care of it, it will take care of you. If you love it, it will love you back. It would never leave you. I was totally convinced of this hypothesis and that conviction was reflected in the way I ran my life. I would go into a relationship but the moment the man became demanding, I would end it, for fear that if would be a threat to my career.

I found my identity in my work. Tessie Tomas was Meldita. Was Bonnie Buendia. Was Miss Margarida. Was Amanda Pineda. Was Miriam Detektor Saanmanmagtago. Was the myriad of personalities I had done for my numerous one-woman shows. In private conversations with close friends, I would gloss over my love life and even Robin, and instead talk endlessly about my shows, the new scripts I was doing, or my forthcoming productions. Everything I talked about was work-related. In my quiet moments, I asked myself: Who is Tessie beyond being an actress-comedienne-writer? Blank. An empty blurb. A dead end.

On that smoggy day in Los Angeles, a flurry of questions crowded my mind. What was I doing there? Did I really have to do this? How could I let go of such a nice man in favor of my career? Was it really worth it? What did I really want? Was I happy? Was this all there was to life? And so on and on and on. I started to get sick physically. I came down with a severe flu that lasted a whole week. At the height of my fever I wrote a mushy letter to my Norwegian friend, saying I wanted him back. That I had come to realize that career was not all there was to life. That I was willing to give up my career and go with him to Norway. After two weeks, I received an angry letter from him. I was saying these crazy things only because my career in Los Angeles had not taken off, he said. He did not believe that I could really give up my work for him.

I RETURNED to Manila in May 1989. By then, the pilot season in Los Angeles had ended. I almost landed the role of a Hispanic rebel opposite Lou Gossett Jr. in a miniseries, but a more Hispanic-looking actress was chosen over me. My agent and Bob Markowitz encouraged me to return the following year. Quite decisively, I said I preferred to pursue my career in the Philippines.

The rest of that year I buried myself in work. In June, I played the coveted role of Candida in "Larawan," the Tagalog version of Nick Joaquin's "A Portrait of the Artist as Filipino." Subsequently, I formalized my company, Megastar Productions, with myself as president, financier, and artist. At the end of each day, I took home a terrible migraine and a lot of office problems, from cash flow to new concepts for shows.

To keep myself busy, I launched a series of one-woman shows for Megastar. But to a certain extent, I also went through a stage of immobility and isolation. I was simply not comfortable having people around me. I withdrew into my own little cocoon. I never returned my friends' calls. I stopped dating and even avoided parties. I turned into a recluse. My best friend was my notebook. Into it I

193

would pour out all my angsts and even my random thoughts. Sometimes I'd do mirror therapy which I had learned in an actors workshop. I would talk to myself in front of a mirror, pulling out of my inner sanctum all my sadness, desperation, anger, and everything else I felt at that moment. The exercise was like purging the demons within me. It cleansed and tranquilized my spirit, lulling me to a restful sleep.

At this stage too, I began visiting my psychologist-friend more frequently. I would confide in her all my crazy thoughts. I told her that I opened my closet one day and was overwhelmed by all the clothes, costumes, and accessories I had accumulated over the years. Did I need all these? If I decided to go to Palawan, all I needed to take along were a few shorts, some shirts, my beloved typewriter, and the many books I had bought but had not found time to read. Yes, I was aching to go to Palawan, my chosen escape route, away from the madness of the city and the neurosis of showbiz work. In a way, I also wanted to escape from Robin, who was beginning to have adolescent problems. Dealing with my crisis and his teenage problems at the same time was a bit too much to handle.

Many times I felt very tired from working too hard. I had been working since I was nine years old. When could I look forward to resting?

I computed my savings to find out how long I could stay jobless and still be able to support Robin's schooling. I figured that if I scrimped in Palawan I could stay there for six months or even a year. Hallelujah! My heart leapt at the sheer possibility. I spoke to my brother Manny, and he and his wife said they were willing to adopt Robin while I was away. My mother was completely shocked to know I wanted to stop working at forty— why, she herself was still working at sixty-three. That made me feel very guilty.

In the meantime, from January to December 1990, I worked like a dog trying to save as much as I could in preparation for my self-imposed sabbatical the following year.

It was not easy. I remember doing a whole new show that would run for two weekends at the Cosmo Bar in October 1990. I was in the depths of my emotional turmoil and did not feel like doing it. But just thinking about office expenses like the phone and power bills, the payroll, and my day-to-day household expenses made me accept the offer. Psyching myself, I started to work on the scripts: a rap number a la MC Hammer for the opening, a spoof of the Iran-Iraq war and the Pinoy workers stranded in the desert, a Meldita and Gerry Expense (a spoof of Imelda Marcos' American, lawyer Gerry Spence) as finale. Great. We had a show.

On opening night, I was RB, my initials for rock bottom, meaning my depression had hit rock bottom. I could not figure out where the depression was coming from. The show did not have any major problems, except for a few snags in the budget. Robin and I did not have any big argument that day. Maybe it was just a buildup of the burnout I had been feeling. I was not really in the mood to act that night. I was distracted. I fumbled my lines as I rehearsed them. I was having cold sweat.

I managed to go through opening night. The place was jampacked. Some people had to be turned away. The show was a success. The audience was rowdy.

On the second night, we had a strange audience. People were smiling but not laughing. The place was full but quiet, or so it seemed to me, as I stood at center stage amid the hot lights. They were |not, crackling with laughter or ad-libbing about the |jokes. They were listening. I got so paranoid about the whole thing that halfway through the show, in the middle of the spoof of the Pinoy workers in Iraq, I felt like I wanted to stop, snap out of the act, and just say: "Look, don't you find this funny? Okay, then let's just stop this crazy act and let's all go home." It was a scene straight out of the movie "Punch Line," when Tom Hanks goes hysterical while doing his stand-up comedy act in front of the top executives of a TV network. This was not the first time it happened to me and I'm sure every performer experiences it from time to time. In my case, I used to handle the situation very well. I would try to rise above the mountain of negative feelings about my audience, trust my material, trust that my audience would be entertained by what I was about to do, and just enjoy the performance.

This time I was scared. I felt I had nothing much to offer my fans. That my comedy was stale. That I was running out of steam. I felt like a tire that had gone flat and could no longer be vulcanized. Or that my battery was getting weak but could not be recharged anymore. I needed changing.

My psychologist reassured me all my feelings were valid. I did not have to be angry with myself. I did not have to be scared. I just had to accept the way I felt. True, it was part of the burnout. There was a part of me which said I had to do the show, but another part of me screamed and protested and wanted to put a stop to what I was doing. My psychologist told me that I had to take a break to integrate the many sides of Tessie that were coming out in my midlife passage. I was confused. I wanted to stop working. But there was Megastar. I had to keep going. I could not bear to lose face. What would Ambie, my personal manager, say? How would my staff feel? What would my colleagues say? That I was a flash in the pan, that I couldn't see my company through? I felt accountable to everyone, except to myself and my innermost feelings. And what timing! Just when I realized I was having a midlife crisis, I decided to put up a company. It was true. I was like a candle being burned at both ends.

My relationship with Robin was becoming strained at this time. He could not understand my mood swings. One minute I was bubbly, cracking jokes. The next minute I would become pensive, clam up and rush to my room where I would lock myself for hours. At times I felt Robin was a burden to me. How difficult it is to raise a teenager alone. How could Robin and I talk about the intimate details of puberty and teenage sexuality? The few times I spoke to his father I told him he should talk with Robin openly about the facts of life. I trust that he did.

Robin was also having tremendous adjustment problems in his first year of high school. He felt that Don Bosco was too technical, too regimented, compared to JASMS where he had spent his grade school years. Two months after school opened, he wanted to quit. We went to my psychologist for a three-way talk. We were able to convince Robin that having some form of therapy would help him. He chose painting.

Robin also resented the fact that I wanted to leave him and go to Palawan. I tried very hard to explain to him what I was going through but it seemed vague to his young mind. What was clear to him was that I was selfish, that all I could think of was myself, that I was dumping him on my brother. I felt angry. I told myself I was entitled to have a crisis. After taking care of him for seven years, I deserved a break. I felt like stealthily packing my things and just leaving without warning. Like a stowaway kid. But I controlled myself. January 1991 was not too far behind.

Three weeks before my fortieth birthday, in October 1990, I was still in a quandary as to how I would celebrate it. Should I throw a big party, as my friends expected me to do? Or should I just quietly slip away to Kuala Lumpur and celebrate it with Julie, one of my best friends, and her family? The year before, I was fantasizing about inviting my top forty friends, renting a private plane that would fly all over Manila while we had a bash inside the aircraft — caviar, champagne, cheese, the works! I decided to have a very low-key celebration. I invited some of my closest friends to a very private dinner at La Gondola restaurant. As I blew out the candles on the surprise birthday cake, I made a strange spiel: "As I turn forty, I feel I'm undergoing a lot of changes. The Tessie you see now is fast evolving. You may or may not like the changes. I hope you will be there to help me go through my transition. And just accept me for what I may turn out to be." I could see the confused look on their faces but I knew that eventually they would understand.

AT THIS POINT I feel I must tell you about some of my friends who are also in midlife and the conversations I have had with them.

Angie is forty-four. She works as marketing directress in a big multinational company. She has been separated from her husband for many years and has raised two lovely children, now aged nineteen and twenty-one. Angie cannot understand why I'm having a midlife crisis. She says she did not experience one and probably never will.

That's because she takes life in stride. She also advises me to always think young. Mind you, she looks thirty-two.

Ada is thirty-eight and was my schoolmate at UP. She feels I'm too intense, that I dissect life to its minutest details. That's why I'm having such a tough time in midlife. With her esoteric background and knowledge of astrology, she insists my being a Scorpio makes me capable of absorbing a lot of pain. She feels I am not ready for a relationship. That I should work on myself first. That my career should not be sacrificed at all cost. That I can have my man eventually but there's no need to get married. A widow, she enjoys her singlehood immensely.

Julie is forty-six and has been one of my closest friends since my advertising days. She was like a beacon of light in those darkest moments when I separated from my husband in 1981. We would have a beer at lunchtime just to get me through a difficult day at the office, especially just a few days after my husband packed up and left me for another woman. Julie feels I have intellectualized my feelings, that I have not allowed myself to feel. She says I don't stay in a relationship because I'm scared of commitment, I'm scared that the man will leave me eventually, and so I leave him first. She believes that I deserve to be happy and that the root of my loneliness in my midlife is the lack of a solid, long-term relationship with a nice man.

Caridad must be in her fifties. She believes that my breakup with my Norwegian friend was predestined. That it was not meant to be. That I was not truly in love with him; otherwise I would be willing to give up my career for him. I was jolted by that observation. She asks me, how do you pray? I pray when I'm in need. What do I pray for? I pray for success in my career. Do I ever pray for my personal happiness? I don't. It's about time you did, she says.

Noni is about thirty-five. He is my yoga teacher. I decided to take up centering exercises through yoga with him upon my psychologist's advice. Through the hatha yoga exercise, I learned proper breathing. I learned that the center of my body is two inches below my navel and that whenever I am caught in a tense situation, I should breathe deeply and concentrate on my body's center to gain equilibrium. Noni has become a good friend of mine. We have long conversations on karma and the natural flow of life. Nothing ever happens by chance, he says, and everyone we meet has a purpose: to enlighten us, to test our convictions, or to change our bad habits.

Through the months that I was taking up yoga and doing meditation, I experienced a marked improvement in myself. I became more relaxed in the office. I had more energy to listen to problems. I maintained my composure even in the worst situations.

I also started to pray hard. I found inner peace by praying in front of the exposed Blessed Sacrament at the Adoration Chapel of Don Bosco Church. I would just kneel there, cry when I felt like crying, or simply lift up to God all my worries and travails. In all humility, I started to pray differently: "Lord, I am so confused. I don't know where my life is going. I realize that you have given me and my career many blessings, but I feel so empty still. I cannot understand myself. I have never prayed for my personal happiness before. It was always for my career. It was always for Robin. But now, in all humility, I ask you, Lord. I need someone who will love me. I need to love again. If it is your will, please let him come into my life. Please help me."

Caridad would have been happy to hear my prayers. Every day, morning and evening, I prayed for my personal life. I did not tell God what to do or how to do it. I never pressured Him to make it happen right away. I simply prayed.

A MONTH LATER, I met Roger. A dear friend arranged a blind date for us. We had dinner in his condominium with a few of his friends. Roger is a British biologist and aquaculture expert working in an international marine institute based in Manila. His job takes him to Bangladesh, Germany, Switzerland, Hungary, and Africa for scientific conferences and follow-ups of his office's many projects.

He loves music and the other arts. The biologist and the comedienne soon found they had a lot in common. In time I became the first person he'd call when he came back from a trip.

But I vacillated, feeling ambivalent about the possibility of another relationship. I was not over my midlife crisis. Not by a long shot. I told Roger about my plans of going to Palawan. He said he'd join me there as soon as he could take a break from his work.

December 1990 was a busy month. There were company parties and sales launches for private companies. I accepted most of the offers, thinking I needed the money for the trip to Palawan. Yes, I still wanted to go to Palawan for a few months even though I was already going out with Roger. I felt he could wait.

On December 20, 1990, I received a shocking letter from him. He said he would not be able to see me in the meantime because of some personal problems. He also hinted that he was uneasy in his job and would consider taking a new assignment somewhere in Europe.

I was speechless. Depressed. Angry. Is this what I get after praying hard for a nice man? After telling myself I'm willing to sacrifice my career if the right man comes along? It wasn't worth it! Just when I thought we'd spend a lovely Christmas together, he writes this awful letter. I felt cheated. Rejected. I knew I would have a lousy Christmas.

A week before Christmas, I received a call from ABS-CBN for the pilot taping of a new sitcom called "Abangan Ang Susunod Na Kabanata." It was to be a satire on three families: the superpoor, the middle class, and the superrich. I would be Barbara Tengco, the neurotic, pill-popping wife of the corrupt Congressman Tengco. I couldn't believe what the executive producer was telling me. It was too good to be true. I felt hyper again. A TV sitcom!

Television work would lift me out of the boredom of stand-up comedy. Would I accept the offer? But what about Palawan? What about my midlife crisis? I had only two days to make a decision. The pilot had to be ready by the last week of December for airing on the first week of January 1991. But what if I suddenly felt my crisis coming on again in the middle of a taping? I might just walk out of the show. I might just decide to fly off to Palawan if I can't handle the pressure. Finally, I took the offer.

I had a chance to go to Palawan for five days before taping started. As I sunbathed at a beach in Puerto Princesa, I felt a great sense of imbalance. I knew I had set my mind on taking a sabbatical in January, so why on earth did I accept the TV offer? I was doing the exact opposite of what I had to do.

I consulted my psychologist about my dilemma. She was also surprised about the turn of events but she agreed that I should take the TV assignment. While a trip to Palawan would have been ideal, the TV work represented the change I was looking for. But she cautioned me not to overwork myself again and to take a break every time I felt burned out.

In February 1991, Roger resurfaced in my life. Over dinner, he explained his plan to hold on to his job and stay longer in Manila. I was skeptical. I felt very protective of myself and my feelings.

That February was a red-letter month. The late morning TV show "Teysi Ng Tahanan" was offered to me. It changed my life. I had to cut down on parties and dates. I had to go to sleep by ten or eleven at the latest and be up by seven in the morning to be at the Channel 2 studio at 9:30 for the Monday-to-Friday show.

My first three months on "TNT" were not good at all. I was always getting sick. Some well-meaning friends told me I was very hyper during the first few weeks. I overprojected and spoke in a loud, shrill voice. I cut my guests short and was more preoccupied with what I would say next instead of listening to them. Every time we had a weak episode, I would complain and cry to Deo, my executive producer. I took personal responsibility for the show and felt un-believably disappointed and let down if the episode did not come up to my standards. I didn't want people to say my show was lousy.

As the months passed, I learned to adjust to the system. Deo was right. If we had a rather weak show on Monday, we still had Tuesday through Friday to recover. I also started to believe in the show and in what I could do as a host. Buoyed by the favorable feedback and the hundreds of fan letters we received every week, I grew more confident of my talent. I also let go of my desire for perfection—in my spiels, in my repartee with my guests. If only a few guests showed up for the day's show, I learned how to live with it. If the topic did not appeal to me, I just let go. Overall, I appeared more relaxed and happy in front of the camera. Whether I was coming down with the flu or struggling with a family problem, I tried to box it in. I learned to say a short prayer before the show and to tell myself "TNT" is only for one hour. "Lord, help me forget my problems for just one hour so I can spread happiness to the millions of housewives watching. I know I can go back to my problems after the show. My fans don't have to know."

Although 1991 kept me busy with "Abangan" and "TNT," I was still able to see Roger regularly. My gut feel told me he is a stable and steady man, a mature person who could handle my immaturity and sporadic attacks of childishness.

Roger has such a calming effect on me. Even as he himself comes from a hectic day at work, with frayed nerves and all, he always asks me how my own day was. He patiently listens to all the gruelling details of my work. At first it was one-way. He'd let me talk on and on about my work and my problems. Later on, I found myself listening to him talk about his own problems and frustrations with his job, his loneliness living away from his two daughters who are in England, his dream of writing books for children to make them more appreciative of nature. In short, we jell. We go to plays and concerts, listen to music at jazz joints, or go to Anilao with his diving buddies. We somehow always have a good time.

These days I have to make sure I have time not only for my daily "Teysi Ng Tahanan" and the weekly "Abangan Ang Susunod Na Kabanata" but also for the various movie assignments offered to me. Learning to say no to certain projects is difficult. My manager always reminds me: *"Iha,* you have it so good now. Make the most of it."

I'M STILL SPEEDING on the highway as far as my career is concerned. I am at an all-time peak, as I have never been before. But I know all this is temporary. Sad to say, a TV show relies primarily on ratings—it can get cancelled with just two weeks' notice. That's how cruel this business is. But now I know that even if the job goes, I will still be whole.

202

I have also learned how to take care of myself, to not always people-please but to make myself my first priority. Knowing that my hands are full with "TNT" and "Abangan," I am able to say no to such activities as speaking engagements or one-woman shows. Despite my crazy schedule, I try to squeeze in some "sanctuary hours," as I call them. If you see me at a coffee shop or a restaurant all by myself, don't wonder why. I do that on purpose. These are the moments when I try to reach my center and enjoy my solitude. That's when I review the past week, plans for the coming week, or the good and bad decisions I've made.

Being a frenetic, high-energy person, I'm always conscious that I have to slow down. When I get into this nasty habit of listing down twenty things I want to do for the day, I lean back and reduce them to the five most important things. That gives me a little more time to relish a phone conversation with a long-lost friend. Or simply to have a little quality talk with Robin about school or his friends. Or a little more time to absorb my maid's problems about housekeeping.

I hammer into myself the adage "I work to live, I don't live to work." A lot of the imbalance and crisis in my midlife has stemmed from my being a work addict. I let my work dictate everything I can or cannot do in my life. I have become notorious with my mother and my brothers for not showing up at family reunions and other major events because of work. I once missed Robin's graduation from art class at the Ayala Museum because I had an emergency taping. I'm not perfect and I cannot promise I can do it one hundred percent of the time. But my batting average as far as fulfilling family commitments go has greatly improved.

I've also learned the hard way that my career cannot give me my identity. I am still in the process of finding the many sides of Tessie. Tessie the actress is just a speck of my totality. There's the woman who wants to be loved and to love back. The child who wants to recapture her childhood. The girl who wants to bum around with friends. Or rally people to a noble cause. Or to help young artists. The self-discovery I am making in midlife is staggering.

Most people say I am looking more relaxed and happy these days.

203

Or that I'm blooming, younger-looking. I feel flattered. And it's not because I've undergone the latest state-of-the-art facial treatment. The relaxed, happy me that people see comes from, pardon the cliché, an inner glow, an inner strength which tells me I will go through midlife a better person, a better friend to my dear Robin, and a better woman to my special friend, Roger. I guess I'm not afraid of commitments anymore. My career is there while I want it, but when I need to make a decision to settle down again, I shall keep an open mind.

Right now, I struggle to find a little more time to discover more about myself over and above being an actress-comedienne-TV host. I know I can do it slowly. Just sharing and writing this article gives me immense gratification that the writer in me is coming out again. One day I shall write a book. It will be about life. About ordinary people. About you and me.

The Women Behind The Book

The Writers

Bernardita A. Azurin (a.k.a. Berni Quimpo), former teacher, magazine publisher and editor, and communication specialist, has no regular job at present and is not in the market for one. What she is busy with is figuring out what to do with the rest of her life.

A native of Vigan, Ilocos Sur, she earned an A.B. degree, major in English and journalism, from St. Paul College of Manila where she was a campus editor. She has spent more than half of her working life as a writer, editor, and publisher. She taught briefly, worked in a newspaper, published and edited several publications, among them the agriculture magazines *Farming Today* and *Agribusiness Watch*, and managed the print and publications department of the Technology and Livelihood Resource Center. She was also for a year a communications associate at Aquatic Farms Limited, a consulting firm based in Honolulu, Hawaii.

Starting with her essay in this book, she is reverting to the use of her by-line in the Sixties in the hope that she "will recapture some of the optimism, bravado, and madness" she believes she exhibited during that period.

Her husband of twenty-five years, Norman F. Quimpo, agrees. So would her son, Leon.

Florina F. Castillo has been principal of the Grade School of St. Scholastica's College, Manila, since 1981. She has a Bachelor of Arts degree, major in English (cum laude), from St. Scholastica's and a master's in educational management from De La Salle University. She is now taking doctoral studies in literature at the University of Santo Tomas.

Among her fellow educators, she is known for having pioneered in gifted education, peace education, and more recently, in interdisciplinary studies at the grade school level.

She writes children's stories and poetry on the side. Recently, she joined Naty Crame Rogers' Philippine Drama Company, a theater for nonprofessionals.

She is married to Jose A. Castillo. They have four children: Jose Flavio, Jose Gabriel, Czarina, and Elizabeth Regina.

Gemma Teresa Guerrero Cruz is a fiction writer, essayist, political analyst, entrepreneur, and jewelry designer. She has a Bachelor of Arts degree, major in foreign service, from Maryknoll College and took her master's on "Estudios Mexico-Estados Unidos" at the Universidad Nacional Autonoma de Mexico.

As Miss Philippines of 1964, when she was not quite twenty-one, she won the Miss International contest in Long Beach, California, but four years later became the first beauty queen to join a politically oriented feminist movement, the Malayang Kilusan ng Bagong Pilipina (Makibaka).

She was director of the National Museum for three years. In 1974 she left the country for Mexico, where she lived until 1989 and where, among other jobs, she was *asistente principal de programacion* at the United Nations Development Programme.

She has written three books: *Makisig the Little Hero of Mactan* , which has become a classic in Filipino children's literature, *Hanoi Diary,* and *Beauty Book for the Filipina.* She has won several awards for short story writing.

In 1991 she established Simoun Jewelry Unlimited Inc., for which she fashions semiprecious jewelry using prehistoric and colonial Philippine designs.

She has two children, Fatimah Carmen and Leon Angel Araneta.

Neni Sta. Romana-Cruz is a free-lance journalist, children's book writer, and educator. As a journalist, her articles have appeared in various periodicals and anthologies. She has written two books for children: *Gabriela Silang* of the Great Lives Series, which won a 1992 National Book Awards citation, and *Why the Piña Has a Hundred Eyes and Other Classic Philippine Folk Tales About Fruits.* As an educator, she heads the Children's Media Center at the International School in Makati and also teaches a mentorship writing program for gifted elementary school students.

She holds a Bachelor of Arts degree, major in English (cum laude), from St. Scholastica's College, Manila, and a master's in English literature from the Ateneo de Manila University. She has also taken postgraduate courses in children's literature at Michigan State University.

She and her husband, Elfren S. Cruz, have three children: Tanya, Roel, and Aina.

Ma. Soledad (Chic) N. Fortich writes a weekly column in the Philippine Daily Inquirer and occasional feature articles in local magazines.

Born in Mambajao, Camiguin, she grew up in Cagayan de Oro City and graduated from Xavier University with a Liberal Arts degree, major in English literature and social sciences. She relocated to Manila with her family in 1986.

She is the author of *ESCAPE!* (the biography of Charito Planas), fourteen Pilipino novellas and three English novels, and has won a Palanca Memorial Award for a three-act play in English. She also won the grand prize in a magazine-sponsored love story contest in 1989.

Born with two genetic conditions, retinitis pigmentosa and optic atrophy, she has only two percent remaining vision in her right eye and zero in her left. Her hearing capacity is less than fifty percent. Nonetheless, she remains active in the Philippine Blind Union, the UN-ESCAP Decade of Disabled Persons Task Force, and the Circle of Mary as a spiritual counselor.

She is married to Thomas J. Fortich. They have two daughters, Maia and

Connie.

Ma. Eloisa (Mariel) N. Francisco is a writer and teacher. She obtained her A.B. in English literature from Maryknoll College and her M.A. in English from the Ateneo de Manila University. She has taught language, literature, Philippine life and culture, and holistic studies at the Ateneo. As English language teaching consultant to the World Health Organization, she has worked with health professionals and teachers of English in China and Vietnam.

She co-authored, with Fe Maria C. Arriola, *History of the Burgis* (GCF Books) which won the Manila Critics Circle National Book Award for history for 1987. She has also written feature articles for various magazines.

A recipient of British Council and Fulbright study and research grants, she has attended the North-South Writers and Publishers Workshop at the Frankfurt Book Fair.

She is married to Jesus P. Francisco. They have four daughters: Nini, Joanna, Ivi, and Resa.

Judette A. Gallares, r.c. is a member of the Philippine Cenacle Community. She is currently based in Cebu City where she is involved in retreat work, spiritual direction, and the faith formation of urban poor women.

She has a commerce degree, major in accounting, from St. Theresa's College, Quezon City, and is a certified public accountant, having passed the government examination for CPAs in 1968. Before entering the Cenacle in 1971, she worked briefly at Operations Brotherhood International and the Asian Development Bank.

She holds a master's in religious studies from Fordham University in New York and a certificate in biblical spirituality from the Catholic Theological Union in Chicago, Illinois.

She is the author of four books, all of them published by Claretian Publications: *Following God's Call, Praying with Job, Praying with Jonah,* and *Images of Faith.* She has also composed religious songs.

Margarita Go Singco-Holmes, Ph.D. is a clinical psychologist with an A.B. from the University of the Philippines, an M.P.H. from the University of Hawaii, and a doctorate from the Ateneo de Manila University.

She is the author of five books: *Life, Love, Lust; Passion, Power, Pleasure; Roles We Play in Family Life; A Different Love;* and *Sexy, Saucy, Spicy.* She writes a column, "Bodymind," in The Manila Times six days a week. Until recently, she hosted a segment in the television show "Teysi Ng Tahanan" and did six seasons of "No Nonsense with Dr. Holmes," the very first TV program in the Philippines to focus on psychological issues.

She has one daughter, Alexandra.

Marra PL. Lanot is a poet and essayist in English and Filipino. She has won two Palanca Memorial Awards: second prize for her first book of poems, *Sheaves of Things Burning,* and first prize for an essay. She has also received a Talaang Ginto prize for two poems in Filipino and the Catholic Mass Media Award for her column in the defunct *Midweek* magazine. Her poems have been anthologized here and abroad.

In 1992, she published *Dream Sketches*, a compilation of personality profiles she has written for several magazines.

An English and comparative literature major at the University of the Philippines, she is currently taking a graduate course in Spanish, also at the UP.

She is married to Jose F. Lacaba. They have a son, Kris.

Carolina (Bobbie) S. Malay is a free-lance editor and writer. She has an A.B. degree, major in English, from the University of the Philippines and a graduate diploma from the French Press Institute in Paris.

After graduating from the UP and until she left for Paris, she worked at the *Evening News* and *The Manila Times*. Upon returning from Paris in the early Seventies, she chose to join the staff of the Times' Filipino newspaper, Taliba.

When martial rule was imposed in 1972, she went underground and, with Times colleague Satur Ocampo, started a life together and a family. She remained in the underground for eighteen years, except for a few months during the cease-fire for the peace talks in 1986.

She and Ocampo were arrested in 1988 and released in 1991 after two years and three months in prison.

Since her release, she has been writing, editing, and teaching journalism courses at the UP College of Mass Communication.

She collaborated with her mother, the late Paula Carolina S. Malay, on a Filipino translation of Carlos Bulosan's *America Is in the Heart*. Their book, *Nasa Puso Ang Amerika*, was released by Anvil in 1993.

The Ocampos have two children, Silahis and Antonio.

Asuncion David Maramba is a college professor, book editor, columnist, and homemaker. She graduated from St. Theresa's College, Manila with two degrees, Bachelor of Arts and Bachelor of Science in Education (both summa cum laude), and took her M.A. at the Ateneo de Manila University.

For many years, she was the English department chair and associate professor at Scholastica's College, Manila. She has also been a professional lecturer at De La Salle University but now teaches at San Carlos Seminary and Rogationist Seminary.

She is the author of the following books: *Companion to Shakespeare, Outline History of Philippine Literature in English, Practical Household Management,* and *View from the Middle*. As a book editor, she has done *Philippine Contemporary Literature, Early Philippine Literature,* the Cacho Hermanos *Shakespeare Series, New Integration, National Communication Arts I; Ninoy Aquino, the Man the Legend, On the Scene* (the Philippine Press Coverage of the 1986 Revolution), and most recently, *Six Modern Filipino Heroes*.

She has contributed feature articles and commentaries to various newspapers and magazines and has written columns in several publications.

She received the Catholic Mass Media Award for best feature writing in 1986 and a Catholic Authors Award in 1992.

Recently, she completed the Basic Management Program at the Asian Institute of Management.

She and her husband, Federico K. Maramba, have four children: Rita, Ricky, Dina, and Fritz.

Imelda M. Nicolas chairs the National Commission on the Role of Filipino Women and is a columnist of *Malaya*.

She majored in the humanities (magna cum laude) at St. Theresa's College, Manila, and took graduate studies in art history at the Columbia University in New York and in mass communication at the University of the Philippines.

She is the president of the Ugnayan ng Kababaihan sa Pulitika and Women in Nation-Building and past president of the Alliance of Women for Action and Education (AWARE). Since 1988, she has chaired the Office of the President's Committee for Women's Concerns.

She was assistant appointments secretary at the Office of the President during the Aquino administration and was simultaneously chief of staff of the office of Sen. Agapito Aquino.

In 1991, she organized the Second Women's GO-NGO National Congress, the First National Congress of Women in Electoral Politics, and the seminar on "Filipino Women's Guide to Winning Elections in the '90s."

She has never married.

Alice (Peanuts) A. Pañares has been teaching art to both children and adults for more than twenty-five years.

An A.B. graduate of St. Theresa's College, Manila, she taught for many years at the Ateneo Grade School in Loyola Heights and in 1979 established a Children's Art Gallery at the Greenhills Creative Child Center.

As president of the Philippine Art Educators Association and regional head of the Southeast Asia Pacific Region of INSEA (International Society for Education Through Art), she has conducted workshops and seminars for art teachers in different provinces of the Philippines and in ASEAN countries.

At present she teaches art to high school students at the International School in Makati.

She has one daughter, Zeena, by the late Raul Pañares.

Ma. Agnes O. Prieto writes a weekly column in The Sunday Chronicle and runs a public relations outfit. She is also a businessperson engaged in countryside development. She has been a teacher and a diplomat.

She completed her college studies at Assumption College and took graduate courses in psychology at the Ateneo de Manila University.

She has published two books: *The Whims of Time*, a collection of her short stories, and *Under My Skin*, a compilation of her essays in the *Chronicle*.

She has four children: Francis, Xavier, Friena, and Miguel.

Teresita Hermosa Tomas, better known as Tessie Tomas, is one of the Philippines' best known comediennes and film and television actresses.

She graduated from the University of the Philippines Institute (now College) of Mass Communication, where she majored in broadcasting.

Immediately after college, she plunged into advertising, starting as a copywriter trainee in several agencies. In 1978, McCann-Erickson made her the first Filipino creative director.

Three years later, after a decade in advertising, she made a drastic career move. She became a television star via the weekly entertainment show "Champoy." From there, she launched a series of one-woman spoof shows, starting in 1982 as the character Amanda Pineda. She followed this up with a risqué Brazilian play with a political message, "Miss Margarida's Way." Her choice of material marked a breakthrough in Philippine theater.

An even bigger success was "Meldita," a political satire based on the life of Imelda Romualdez Marcos. The show ran for over a year and reached as far as Los Angeles, San Francisco, and New York.

In 1988, she tried television drama with the miniseries "A Dangerous Life," in which she again played the former first lady. For that role, she was named one of the finalists for best actress in a TV miniseries in the American Cable Entertainment Awards of Hollywood the following year.

In 1992, she won a best actress award in the Metro Manila Filmfest.

She hosts the Monday-to-Friday TV show "Teysi Ng Tahanan" and stars in the weekly sitcom "Abangan Ang Susunod Na Kabanata." She has won the Star Award as best daily TV talk show host twice — in 1991 and 1992. "Teysi Ng Tahanan" has also won a Star Award as best daily TV show.

She has one son, Robin.

The Book Designer

Joanne de León is a free-lance book illustrator and designer and graphic artist. A painting major at the University of the Philippines College of Fine Arts, she started doing illustrations for organizations and for Cacho Publishing even while still a student.

Her first children's book, *Two Friends, One World,* for Cacho Hermanos led to a series of coloring books for Anvil Publishing. She has done other children's books such as *The Carabao Turtle-Race and Other Classic Philippine Animal Folk Tales* and a cookbook for Bookmark, and *Nawawalang Araw* and *The Environmental Alphabet* for Cacho Hermanos.

At 27, she has already won several awards: the Philippine Board on Books for Young People's Illustrator's Prize (1990), the Goethe Institut workshop prize (1990), and the NOMA Concours Encouragement Prize (1992).

The Cover Painter

Barbara (Tweetums) C. Gonzalez, though busy as president of J. Romero and Associates and concurrent president of Coca-Cola Foundation Philippines, Inc., writes a column, "Real Things," for The Sunday Times and lectures on the essay at the Ayala Museum.

She has authored a book on single parenthood, *How Do You Know Your Pearls Are Real?* (Anvil Publishing 1991), which won a National Book Award from the Manila Critics Circle.

In 1993, she mounted at the Ayala Museum her first exhibition of watercolors which she called "First Blush." Among the paintings in that show was her self-portrait, which appears on the cover of this book.

She has four children: Risa, Sarri, Panjee, and Gino.

The Editor

Lorna Kalaw-Tirol has been a journalist since 1968, the year after her graduation from St. Theresa's College, Quezon City, with an A.B. degree major in English and journalism. She started as a deskperson at The Manila Chronicle, moved to the Philippines Free Press as a copyreader and occasional feature writer, became associate editor of the Asia-Philippines Leader, and worked briefly in Hong Kong as a sub editor at the weekly regional newspaper The Asian and Asian News Service. Back in Manila, she spent three years as associate editor, first of Woman's Home Companion and then of General Motors' Goodman magazine, before deciding to free-lance so as to have more time for her growing children. Since returning to full-time journalism in 1982, she has been associate editor of Panorama magazine and of the revived Manila Times, editor of Sunday Times Magazine, associate editor of the post-EDSA Manila Chronicle, managing editor of Mr. & Ms., opinion editor of Manila Standard, and Manila coordinator of Women's Feature Service. She is now the editor of the Sunday Inquirer Magazine.

She co-edited the books *Dictatorship and Revolution: The Roots of People's Power* and *1992 and Beyond: Forces and Issues in Philippine Elections* and edited *Kudeta* and *Remembrance: St. Theresa's College 1921-1980.*

She has taught high school and college students and conducted journalism workshops for children.

She sits on the board of directors of the Philippine Center for Investigative Journalism, which she helped found in 1989.

She and her husband, Vicente G. Tirol, have two sons, Jo-Ed and Paulo.